Improv!

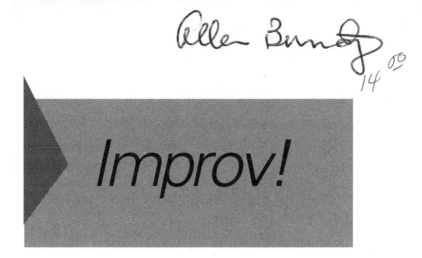

Improv!

A Handbook
for the
Actor

Greg Atkins

HEINEMANN
Portsmouth, NH

Heinemann
A division of Reed Elsevier Inc.
361 Hanover Street   Portsmouth, NH 03801–3912
Offices and agents throughout the world

Distributed in Canada by Reed Books
Canada, 75 Clegg Road, Markham, Ontario L6G 1A1.

Editor: Lisa A. Barnett
Production: Alan Huisman
Text design: George H. McLean
Cover design and illustration: T. Watson Bogaard
Printed on acid-free paper

Library of Congress Cataloging-in-Publication Data

Atkins, Greg.
  Improv! : a handbook for the actor / Greg Atkins.
      p.   cm.
    ISBN 0-435-08627-8
    1. Improvisation (Acting)   I. Title
  PN2071.I5A84   1993
  792'.028—dc20   93-27091
                                                                        CIP

Printed in the United States of America
98 97   DA   5

To my parents,
for always being there for me

To JoAnne and the Fools, *Chris and the* Feet

To Diane Doyle,
for the "playground" she has provided
me the last fifteen years,
"Improv is our life"

To my students,
the hundreds of actors who have allowed
me to take them on a journey without end

And, of course, to The Ladies,
who give me life, love, and passion

Contents

10 Advanced Exercises   103

Preface

I began teaching improvisation in a rented dance studio, armed only with the Viola Spolin classic, *Improvisation for the Theater*. To be totally honest, my only teaching credentials at the time were the reading of one book and an intense passion to create theatre. I had no idea what I was doing. Innocence, however, can be strength, and like any good improvisationalist I made my methods of instruction up as I went along—making mistakes, making discoveries, and most important, making theatre. There were twenty-five students in that first class, and from among them I developed a thirteen-member performing group that created completely improvised shows based on audience suggestion.

Every show was a one-of-a-kind performance. Each show was exciting, challenging, and most of all, fun. Were we scared? Yes. Did we fail at times? Yes again. But we succeeded most of the time, and we had a hell of a good time trying.

It was during these first improvisational experiences that I discovered a basic truth about myself. I am drawn to the freedom of improvisation—no script, no director, nothing but a group of actors creating relationships, conflicts, dialogue, plot, songs, even complete musicals, off the top of our heads. It was easy for me to get caught up in the passion of the emotions, the give-and-take, the energy of the ensemble, as our stories unfolded. I felt a rush of adrenalin every time I stepped onstage. Improvisation is exciting and addictive. From it I acquired self-discipline and confidence in my abilities as an actor.

From then on, improvisation was an important element in everything I did as an actor. When I was appearing in

Summer and Smoke, the actress playing Nellie suggested that we improvise some of the scenes only referred to in the play so she could use them in her emotional recall. The director of a production of *Godspell* asked us to improvise stage business and characters that weren't in the script. As part of an audition for a TV commercial I was asked to mime a soft drink can, pretend to drink from it, and then watch as the imaginary can flew out of my hand, zipped around the room, and buzzed my head. In addition, there were all those times I had to replace an actor with only a few hours notice. In acting, improvisation becomes part of your life.

I also discovered that improvisation made my directing, writing, and teaching more dynamic, passionate, and enjoyable. Improvisation opens an actor up to new ideas, feelings, and concepts and expands mental boundaries, things vital to keeping the mind flexible and strong.

Since that first class, I have performed with other improv groups and taught hundreds of actors and playwrights—amateur and professional—how to liberate spontaneity, think quickly on their feet, enhance creativity, and make more exciting dramatic choices.

How important is improvisation? There are only three areas in which improvisation will help you: auditioning, performing, and living.

Don't think about it; just do it.

Enjoy.

Introduction

This book is designed for use by both actors and directors/teachers. No matter where an actor's interest lies—stage, television, or film—these concepts and exercises will enhance performing skills. The director/teacher can use these exercises to train actors to overcome problems encountered in auditions, rehearsals, and performance.

If you are experienced in improvisation or theatre, many of the exercises in this book will be familiar. Some are acting workshop staples. Some come from books I've read or classes I've taken, and quite a few I've invented myself (at least I think I invented them).

These exercises are fun to do, and the actors should enjoy themselves. Don't misunderstand me—the exercises should be taken seriously. But I find that learning happens more quickly in an energetic, enjoyable workshop environment. Spontaneity and creativity don't emerge as easily in a serious, scholarly atmosphere. Improvisation is the jazz of theatre.

Most of the exercises here will work wonderfully. Some won't, at least not all the time and not for everyone. One year I had the unique experience of teaching improvisation to grades kindergarten through college—some of the students in my college classes were in their fifties—and I found that whatever the age, no one does these exercises perfectly to begin with. Many of the exercises will be wildly popular, and the actors will ask for them in every class. Others will be considered unimportant, and the actors will yearn to move on. Give all the exercises a try and try them again and then try them a third time. Even some of my "failproof" exercises have failed on occasion. So go slowly and build a good foundation with the beginning exercises before you move on to the more advanced ones. It also never hurts to go back and review some of the basics when you notice your improvisations are getting sloppy.

Throughout this book, the term *actor* refers to both males and females. *Actor* is a genderless label in the same way that *doctor* applies to both men and women (there are no doctresses, medical or otherwise). I'll use the word *actress* only if I need to make a gender-specific remark.

Some workshop outlines are given at the end of this book, but these are only suggestions. Each group of actors has different strengths, weaknesses, and needs that can be addressed only by tailoring the exercises to the class.

1 The Basics

"Just give it a bash!"
Laurence Olivier's advice to actors

Improvisation.

The mere thought of having to improvise is enough to send most actors screaming into the night. Actually, improvisation is not that difficult. All you have to do is make up your own dialogue; block your own scene; create your own plot; develop a fully realized character; make your environment seem real; introduce a conflict; and include a beginning, a middle, and an end, complete with climax and denouement. And you must do all of this while the other actors are trying to do the same things in different ways.

"Oh, is *that* all!" you may be saying to yourself.

Actually, no. There's even more to it than that.

Ironically, to become good at improvisation, you need to train and rehearse for it. You need to develop the skills, control, confidence, mental agility, trust, and spontaneity that allow you to improvise. Even though improvisation is "making it up as you go along," you need training to know where you are going.

Improvisation is a vital tool for training actors. I have never been to an audition or a play rehearsal, or directed a show, that did not require some sort of improvisation.

Through improvisation you can learn to speed up the thought process, enhance the imagination, and avoid the deadly "brain freeze." As a result, you can make faster choices at auditions, make more creative choices in scene work, and have more confidence in your performances.

This chapter describes some common obstacles to learning improvisation and explains some of the basic concepts that are important to actors even before they walk onto a stage.

The "I Can't" Quotient

The very first hurdle in improvisational training is the "I can't" quotient. While attempting the exercises in this book you may feel the urge to say "I can't think that fast!" or "I can't do this exercise" or "I can't think of six different non-green vegetables." With this kind of thinking, you turn off or block your thought processes. Rather than concentrating 100 percent on the exercise, you create an insurmountable obstacle that gives you an excuse to fail. When you say, "I can't," what you are really saying is "I won't try."

What causes the "I can't" quotient? You have been told *you can't* since the day you were born. You can't hit people, talk in school, touch the stove, eat before meals, or burp out loud. Every child at one time or another has complained, "Gosh, I can't do anything!" And it's true that for their safety and their assimilation into society, children need rules about "proper" ways of behavior.

Then you walk into an acting class and the director/teacher tells you, "Forget all the crap you've been told since you were born and be free!" When you're instructed to "take that chair you're sitting on and sit on it in a new way," you respond, "I can't sit on the back of the chair." "Show your emotions!" ("I can't be a crybaby.") "Your partner is your sister and you are incredibly angry! Yell at her!" ("I can't yell at my sister.") "Talk to your partner as if you are a snake and she is a mouse." ("I can't be a snake; snakes don't talk.") "Get your mind working faster!" ("I can't think any faster.")

It's difficult to break down years of barriers and just let go. I had a student in my class who, no matter how easy or complex an exercise, would insist she couldn't do it—sometimes before I had described the exercise! Of course she always fulfilled her prophesy. This is a mental block that no one needs. So we'd start over, she'd try again, and eventually she *could* do it.

If you say you *can't* do something, I guarantee you *won't be able* to do it. At least not at first. Give up your "I can't" and "I won't" and "I don't know" and allow yourself to *try*. It may be uncomfortable for awhile, but "give it a bash." Be a little off balance. Allow yourself to be less than brilliant for once. Making mistakes is an important part of learning any new skill. The more you rehearse these exercises, the easier they become. Keep an open mind and try the best you can. If you fail, you fail. Try again. Getting rid of self-imposed obstacles is a major step in becoming a better actor.

Risking

Remember learning to ride a bicycle? How often we fell? Finally, after hours or days of practice, we could ride alone without weaving into a tree. Most of us were satisfied with this achievement. We could get from point A to point B on our bikes without any problem. But a few kids would keep on experimenting, doing "wheelies," coasting with their hands off the handlebars, or riding backwards. And there was that one kid who went even further—learning to do handstands, peddle with someone perched on his shoulders, ride his bike across a tightrope. That kid used the same bicycle as the rest of us but created new and interesting ways to ride it.

The same thing applies to acting. Some actors are content to get from point A to point B. There's nothing special about them, just more actors playing it safe. Others experiment a bit and *seem* to be creative, but they rely on a standard bag of tricks. Finally, there are those actors who have the passion to create, to explore, to take risks. These are the actors who constantly surprise us with their abilities and their courage.

Be the kid who attempts ever more innovative feats. Take the risk.

Fear of Failure

Since childhood, most of us have tried to do things "correctly." Making mistakes means being embarrassed, feeling foolish, and sometimes experiencing pain. As adults and as actors, we still try to avoid making mistakes. However, you are not going to succeed in doing these exercises perfectly the first few times you try them. Don't give up! Mistakes are part of learning. It is much better to attempt new things and possibly fail in a workshop environment than during an audition, in front of an audience, or while shooting a film.

This book and these exercises are your workshop, your laboratory. Here you will always have another chance. The world outside the workshop is not so forgiving. So take a chance. What's the worst that can happen? Embarrassment? Having to try again with the possibility of getting better? Improvisation is not brain surgery. No one dies if you make a mistake.

Brain Freeze

An apt name for a common problem. All actors experience it. You're doing a scene, you've been given your cue, and suddenly . . . NOTHING! Zip. Nada. White noise. No matter how hard you try to think, your brain has hung the "Out to Lunch" sign on your cerebral cortex. You begin to panic. "Think! Think! Think!" you say to your brain. Your brain, in a valiant attempt to make things right, conjures up images of the high school prom, comments on how blue your scene partner's eyes are, and transmits an overpowering urge to vomit so you'll have a physical excuse for getting the hell off the stage. You stand frozen in fear, praying for the curtain to come down, for another actor to save you, or for death, whichever is quickest.

Or consider the inevitable request, "So tell me a little about yourself." When invited to talk about the one thing in the world you're an expert on, you freeze up or blather on about your hobby of collecting cocktail napkins.

Or the look you know the director sees in your eyes (not unlike the eyes of a fawn caught in the headlights of a car) when you audition for a role you didn't prepare for. It all comes down to the dreaded "brain freeze."

Brain freeze is a panic reaction. The brain blanks out and we are unable to think. Improvisational training can virtually eliminate brain freeze by getting the mind to loosen up and keep thinking.

Concentration

Concentration is critical for an actor. From the moment you walk into the theatre, to the moment you stand in your dressing room with applause ringing in your ears, your job requires 110 percent of your concentration. The stress an actor undergoes onstage is equivalent to the stress of an Air Force test pilot. Sweaty palms, dry throat, pounding heart, butterflies in your stomach—the body and mind react the same way whether facing a life-or-death situation or Act 1, Scene 1. The energy, concentration, and control required for acting is astounding. You can't let up on your concentration even for a minute. If you do, your lines leave, your character leaves, and eventually the audience leaves.

Quick Thinking

In improvisation you are *living in the moment* and making choices based on who you are, where you are, and what you are doing. As an actor you strive to accomplish this in rehearsed plays, yet this also is exactly what one does in improvisation. Thinking quickly on your feet, accessing information from your mental Rolodex, and instantly responding to the unfolding scene requires some complex mental aerobics. To do this with any success, you must speed up your thought process to keep up with, if not ahead of, the scene. Listening, analyzing, acting and reacting, making decisions, skimming from one idea to another, and instantly responding can only be accomplished through exercises and rehearsal.

Mental Agility

Mental agility is the ability to move quickly and nimbly from idea to idea, and to adjust to the information that is discovered as the improvisation evolves. It's the quick comprehension and ready response to changes in the scene. In coping with new and changing situations, you must be able to look at one problem in a variety of ways—as actor, director, and playwright—and do it all in a very short time.

Your mind, like your body, benefits from exercise. The exercises in this book will make the mind stronger and more flexible. The further you push your mind, the more extraordinary things it will do.

Three-dimensional and Abstract Thinking

Three-dimensional thinking is a multilevel awareness of the scene. As an actor you must be aware of everything that is occurring onstage. You must know your lines, your character, and your blocking. You must instinctively wait for the laughs to die down, find your light, smoke convincingly, make sure the safety is off on the prop gun, and hit your musical notes. You must check your spacing in the dance number, quickly change your costume and your character, maintain your accent, pick up the glass that happened to fall off the table, and be conscious of the other actors as well. This is daunting enough stuff in a rehearsed play, but it becomes even more complicated in an improvised scene. The secret is not to try to do it all at once (even if that were possible) but to process this continual barrage of information and to quickly and easily move from one thought or choice to the next.

Whereas three-dimensional thinking occurs on many different levels, abstract thinking deals with an element of the scene in a surprising or nontraditional way. It's turning the concepts over in your mind, looking at them from different angles and being selective in your choices. When your acting partner hands you sealing wax, wax your ceiling; if your partner asks you to dance, remind him that mermaids don't dance much but you'd love to learn; when your partner hands you lemons, turn them into used cars.

Spontaneity

We see spontaneous behavior all the time in children. A child says to a stranger, "You're fat." While it may not be socially acceptable, it is a spontaneous act—the child saw, thought, and spoke. As adults, however, we go though life consciously stopping our thought processes and squelching our impulses. This is a good idea for society in general (we need fewer people impulsively climbing clocktowers with deer rifles), but it's important that actors get in touch with the natural, unself-conscious act of creating. Basically, this means trusting your gut instincts and going with them.

Preconceiving

Don't. Don't think about what you're going to do before you do it. Let the ideas unfold naturally within the context of the exercise or scene. Preconceiving is a panic response or a conscious attempt to be clever. Trust that you will be able to improvise with whatever is thrown your way. It may take awhile, but when it does you'll be surprised at how brilliant you can be without even trying.

Censoring

To be spontaneous you must avoid censoring yourself. This takes us back to the "I can't" quotient. Let's say your partner holds out her hand and says, "Look at this!" She has given you very little information (and made a rather poor choice). Your choice can make or break this scene. "My what a pretty flower!" is safe, but perhaps you could find something more exciting that would spark some ingenious improvising. "Madeline, return my penis to me at once!" might well begin a rather exciting scene. Or "A human head!?! Oh,

Umballa, this is the best birthday ever!" These specifics help move the scene forward. If you censor yourself ("Oh, I can't say penis," or "Cannibalism isn't funny") you close off some wonderfully spontaneous choices. Avoiding censoring doesn't mean you should start shouting indiscriminate obscenities (although that can turn out to be a fun and very uplifting exercise). It means not blocking the creative process.

2 Preparation

Rehearsal

When you first learned to drive a car, you probably had trouble mastering everything. You had to remember to buckle your seat belt, turn the key, adjust the mirrors, release the brake, put the car in drive, watch out for the dog, use your turn indicator, avoid other cars, accelerate, watch your speed, obey the laws, try not to listen to your father complain about your driving—in short, to pay attention to a thousand and one things that seemed determined to distract you from driving safely to your destination. And God forbid the car you were learning to drive had a stick shift!

Now, however, having "rehearsed" driving awhile, you get into the car and the only thing you think about is what music to listen to and how much gas you have.

Think of your first attempt at the exercises in this book as your first rehearsal with them. You have to do them over and over until you feel comfortable doing them, and then continue doing them until they become second nature. With rehearsal comes mastery, and with mastery comes self-confidence.

The Voices of Choices

During improvisations you are constantly required to make choices. A good improvisational actor has many choices to call upon during the course of a scene. No matter what the situation—an exercise, a rehearsal, or an improvised scene—the best choice is the one that:

- Works within the context of the scene.
- Remains true to the character(s).
- Furthers the plot.
- Does not negate previously accepted information.

The basic rule about choice is, does the choice help or hinder the scene? In other words, does it further the *who* (characters), *what* (plot), *where* (setting), *when* (year, season, day, time), *why* (motivation), and *how* (action)? Also remember that there can be more than one "best" choice.

Your choices are what will make or break a scene. Safe choices make for boring conflicts. "Gosh, Norma, you sure look nice tonight" is boring, and unless the actor playing Norma comes up with an interesting choice, the most we can expect is a nice, safe scene. "Norma, keep bailing!" is more powerful and lends itself to a strong conflict. This is not to say that every choice should be more dramatic than the last—you still must be true to the scene—but interesting choices make for interesting scenes.

I am often amazed at the dull, repetitive choices I see at auditions. Thirty actors doing the same thing over and over. Not one spark of inspiration or originality. No one taking a risk. No one showing any imagination. These exercises will help you make faster, more creative, and more interesting choices.

Conflict

Can you imagine how dull life would be without conflict? Even though we sometimes feel we could use a little less conflict in our lives, acting without conflict is uninteresting.

Without conflict, the exercises in this book will become tiring and worthless, and the scenes boring and pointless. Conflicts are deeply tied to emotions and wants and can be as simple as "Where should we go to dinner?" or as strong as "The only answer is to put your children in foster care." The idea of putting your children in foster care readily elicits an emotional response—everything from "Thank God, I no longer have to put up with those brats!" to "Over my dead body!" But even something as innocuous as "Where should we go to dinner?" can create a powerful conflict. Possible responses range from "Why do I have to make all the decisions?" to "Anyplace but your ex-husband's restaurant." If you don't care what happens there will be no conflict. Many scenes and exercises will have more than one conflict, but there is always at least one.

No

Saying no stops the action, stops the ideas, stops the story, and is basically a poor choice. I actually witnessed this exchange in an improvised scene:

ACTOR 1: Chris Best? Chris Best! Do you remember me? Artie! Thirty-first Armored Division! You saved my life! How the hell are you?
ACTOR 2: No, sorry, I'm not Chris Best.

Unfortunately, *everyone* was sorry that actor made the choice not to be Chris Best. The scene, needless to say, came to a screeching halt. Saying no and thereby negating previously established information prevents the scene from moving forward. Once a statement has been made, you must deal with it. At times you may want to adapt or elaborate on the information you have been given. This is easily accomplished. Get in the habit of saying yes *and*—or yes *but*. That way, you accept the information *and* continue the give-and-take.

ACTOR 1: Pardon me, but your shoes are on fire.
ACTOR 2: Yes, and you'll find it's one of the big disadvantages of being in hell, but I'm wearing my asbestos pants. I should be okay until my socks ignite.

To create a conflict, you will need to provide an obstacle, but this is still not saying no.

ACTOR 1: Karen, put the gun down.
ACTOR 2: Not until your divorce is final, Edward. Go on, pick up the phone.

Actor 2's choice, while not compliant with Actor 1's choice, wasn't a no, it was a yes-but-first-I'll-create-a-conflict.

Empathy

In improvisation, as in acting in general, the ability to empathize with the characters and the situations enhances the quality of an actor's work. Whereas sympathy is feeling sorry for someone, empathy is sharing another's feelings. For example, sympathy is seeing someone stub her toe and feeling bad for her; empathy is actually experiencing the sensation of the toenail's being bent back—feeling it pull away from the skin and seeing the blood well up under the nail. (You probably have felt some empathy just by reading this!)

Empathy. Isn't that what actors *want* to feel for their characters? Isn't that what we want the *audience* to feel for our characters? We try to understand who our characters are and why they do what they do, and in turn we look inside ourselves to see if we can empathize. If we can't, we must dig deeper into both the character and ourselves. We seek the connection between actor and character by research, experience, and empathy. Because we can empathize, we don't have to kill someone to know what it feels like to be a murderer; we've all felt—in some microscopic way—the urge to kill. Empathy allows us to understand other humans (and even animals) and as actors, to mirror them.

You must empathize. You must care. If you don't, you won't get far in acting or in life. At best you will be a purely technical actor; at worst your acting will be unbelievable. The best actors have a deep level of empathy.

Specifics

When making a choice, specifics are more interesting than generalities. "Nice car" is a dull choice. "Wow, a 1939 Rolls Royce Wraith!" is not only specific, but says something about your character and adds realism to the scene.

Serious vs. Comic Scene Work

Whether a scene is funny or serious, the same improvisational ability applies. The director/teacher should require complete concentration and commitment to the scene no matter what form it takes. Encouraging cheap laughs, breaking character, and going for the joke should all be squelched. Such maneuvers don't help the scene and will destroy the trust among the actors. Focus on doing quality work, whether serious or comic.

A standard improv exercise is to have everyone do a scene based on one word. No other information is given. In one class we did this exercise using the word *love*. In one scene, two male prisoners were saying goodbye because one was being paroled. They were in love, and the prisoner being paroled didn't want to leave. The two discussed how the parolee could get arrested again so they could be reunited. In another scene, two women were playing tennis ("Score? Love–15!") and struggling to understand where the love had gone in their marriages. The prisoner scene was very funny, the tennis scene rather sad. Which was the better scene? Neither. Both were effectively improvised scenes. Strive for variety. If you do well at comedy, try something serious, and vice versa.

Side Coaching

Side coaching is coaching the actors from the sidelines while they are doing their scenes. Depending on how the actors feel about it, side coaching can be either instructive or annoying.

I use side coaching primarily during warm-up exercises (Faster! Don't think! Concentrate on the exercise!). I do this to keep the actors focused on what they need to achieve. But during scene work, I keep side coaching to a minimum. No one will be at auditions giving actors helpful hints from the sidelines. No one will call out instructions from the audience when they're onstage. (Though wouldn't it be nice to be able to do that during particularly bad productions?) As a director/teacher, slowly wean actors from side coaching as they become more proficient at improvisation. Use the discussion following a scene to comment on the strengths and weaknesses of the work.

Mime

The exercises in this book should be done without props or costumes unless they are specifically called for. I recommend pantomiming everything except chairs, for two reasons: you can't possibly have every prop a scene requires, and miming allows you unlimited freedom. If you can think of a prop, you can create it. From guns to nuclear devices to suits of armor to dancing cockroaches—anything can be created through mime.

Creating and maintaining the reality of the mimed props are essential to the integrity of the scene. Once an object is established, *it is there forever.* Nothing will distract an audience faster than seeing an actor walk through an established imaginary door, accidentally crush a previously mimed glass, or sit on another actor's mimed cat. Good use of physical space is one mark of an experienced actor.

Establishing a Scene

Many of the exercises in this book begin with the instruction to "establish a scene." This means establishing a *who* (the characters and their relationships), *what* (a minimal plot idea), *where* (a setting), and *when* for the scene. Examples are a husband and wife discussing their divorce over the breakfast table, and a boss and an employee bumping into each other at a topless bar. Of course, different exercises will have to be set up in different ways. At times only a where will be needed, at other times only a when. And at other times all four ingredients—who, what, where, and when—must be established before the scene can progress to the why and the how.

Discussion

After each exercise, it is important to solicit the participants' observations, impressions, and feelings. Knowing what the exercise provided (or didn't provide) an actor can help the director/teacher evaluate the success of the exercise and give insight into the actor's growth and needs.

Exceptions

There are always exceptions to the rules, especially in improvisation. I have seen experienced actors break every rule of scene development with brilliant results. In one of my favorite improvisations, two actors established a scene without a who, what, where, or when. It wasn't until halfway through that the audience realized the actors were parodying Samuel Beckett's *Waiting for Godot*. I have also winced while less experienced actors negated information, went for the joke, wandered through a scene without a conflict, and basically crashed and burned. In one of my favorites of this type, an actor "shot" a scene partner before either had said a word. The actor who was shot fell "dead," and the gunman, terrified at the thought of having to carry the scene alone, walked offstage. Every scene and every actor's abilities are different. Stick to the basic improvisation guidelines until they become second nature. Only then should you consider bending the rules.

Just Do It!

That seems such an easy concept. It's not. Improvisation takes training and it takes time. Rehearsal will help make the concepts in this book second nature. But the key concept here is, *do it*. Examine it. Think about it (or depending on the exercise, *don't* think about it). Explore it. Analyze it. But most of all, *try it*.

How much you want something is directly related to how hard you are willing to try to achieve it. An acting student I will call Leonard had worked with his partner for two weeks on their final scene when Leonard's partner came to me complaining that Leonard wouldn't memorize his lines. I took Leonard aside and gave him some tips on

memorization (Leonard hadn't asked me for any help because it wasn't that important to him). But as the day of the
final approached, Leonard still didn't know his lines. So,
another chat with Leonard, in which he told me he didn't
think he would be able to do the final scene. I reminded him
that his inability to learn his lines would effect not only his
grade but his partner's grade as well. (No one can act across
from someone calling "Line!" every ten seconds.) When this
didn't seem to impress Leonard, I tried a different approach.
I reminded him that he was on scholarship and that an F in
my class would mean his funds would come to an abrupt
halt. His eyes got wide, he picked up his script, and he
walked off with his partner. His final scene, though not the
most exciting performance I'd ever seen, was letter-perfect.

What had happened? Had those memorization tips finally kicked in? Had a semester's worth of my incredible
teaching finally reached him? Of course not. Leonard realized an F in my class would mean financial problems, angry
parents, and embarrassment—"You must be pretty bad to
flunk Beginning Acting!" (It's possible, but tough.)

I had found the way to motivate Leonard. He wanted
that passing grade badly enough to try. Afterward, I asked
him how he had finally managed to memorize the scene.
His answer? "I just did it."

Are you one of those people who wait until the last
minute to do something? The work is due Thursday, and
you finish it Wednesday night (or worse, Thursday morn-
ing)? Maybe you researched the project all week but waited
until you felt the tug of the clock, the growing tension, and
that rush of adrenalin before starting. If so, you know the
feeling of just doing it.

If, on the other hand, you tend to get things done
weeks before they're due, if you prepare in advance, if you
never do anything without thinking it through, then letting

go and just doing it will be a challenge. But keep at it, because soon it will become second nature. There will come a moment, after all the time you've spent on exercises and improvised scenes, when everything comes together and you tap into your spontaneous source of inspiration. The scene will create itself, and afterward you won't quite know how you did it, just that you did.

So just do it.

3 Getting Started

 *Introduction Circle*
(Group Exercise)

Have the actors sit in a circle and one by one tell a little about themselves. Make sure they focus on who they are and not just on their job, spouse, pets, and hobbies. These things are important, but keep the actors on track by also asking why they are taking improvisation, what they hope to learn, what got them interested in acting, and similar questions. After each actor has talked for a couple of minutes, allow the class to ask questions. Keep the questioning brief and then move on to the next actor. Complete the exercise by telling the class something about yourself.

DISCUSSION

Introduction circle is a good exercise for the first day of class because it allows the actors to get to know one another. Each actor comes to class expecting something different. Each is fearful and feels a little vulnerable. This exercise gets people to open up, brag about accomplishments, and relate to others in the class.

This is also a good time to deal with administrative issues, such as objectives of the class, what to wear, good places to park, and how to contact you outside class.

▶ *Name Volleyball*
(Group Exercise)

Divide the class in half and have the two groups position themselves to play a game of volleyball. Instruct the class that in this game, the net and ball are mimed. When the server hits the ball over the net, she must call out the name of an opposing team member. The named player can then either hit the ball to a teammate by calling out the teammate's name, or hit it over the net by calling out an opposing team member's name. If the ball is hit to an opposing player, that player must hit it to a teammate or back over the net while calling out another player's name. As in a real game of volleyball, the players may set up plays by hitting the ball to teammates, but only three hits/names are allowed per side. Act as referee and award points based on standard volleyball rules.

Discussion

Name Volleyball is a good exercise to help the actors memorize names. It also provides a physical warm-up. Make sure the actors strive to make the ball and net believable. If the ball is hit too hard, call out-of-bounds. If someone stumbles over a name, it means he dropped the ball. Remember to rotate the players and servers.

▶ *Name with Action*
(Group Exercise)

Have the actors form a circle. One actor announces her name and creates an action or movement. The next actor must repeat that name and action, then add his own name and movement. This continues around the circle until the last actor, who must repeat all of the other names/actions and add her own. All actors should be given a chance to see whether they can remember the name/action of everyone in the class.

DISCUSSION

Have the actors mirror the names and actions exactly.

► *Name Cheer*
(Group Exercise)

This exercise is the same as Name with Action except that the actors do one action or movement for each letter of their name. Put together, each series of letters looks like a cheer or choreographed dance. As in Name with Action, the actors must remember everyone's name and movements.

4 Trust Exercises

In life trust builds slowly. In acting we don't usually have much time to become comfortable trusting in our fellow actors.

Actors begin by trusting their own skills and their ability to learn and use new ones. You can't be expected to create an exciting scene while worrying about yourself or your partner's abilities and intentions. Trust in yourself will foster self-confidence and allow you to improvise freely. Trust in the ensemble will result in a creative, safe working environment. For these things to occur, trust must be established at the outset.

There is nothing quite so comforting onstage as working with an actor you can count on. There is nothing quite so frightening as being onstage with an actor who has broken your trust. We know from life how difficult it is to build trust in someone and how difficult it is to reestablish a broken trust. Trust builds slowly and is destroyed quickly. Trusting yourself and your fellow actors is the foundation upon which you build your abilities.

The exercises that follow are specifically designed to encourage individual and ensemble trust.

► *Trust Circle*
(Group Exercise)

Have the actors stand in a tight circle. One actor stands in the middle with eyes closed, feet together, arms crossed over the chest, hands on opposite shoulders. The surrounding actors place their hands on the central actor and then say the actor's name in unison. This signals that the exercise has begun.

Slowly and gently the group moves the central actor around the interior of the circle. The central actor must relax, keeping her feet in place, and trust that the other actors will support her weight and protect her. As the central actor relaxes into the exercise, the surrounding actors pull their hands back; those on one side *gently* push the central actor across the circle so that she can "free fall" a few inches before being caught and supported by the actors opposite. Once the central actor has had the chance to relax and enjoy the exercise, the other actors push the central actor upright and again say the actor's name. This signals that the central actor's turn is over and that she can open her eyes.

DISCUSSION

The Trust Circle works best with groups of eight to twelve. Be very careful to ensure that the central actor's trust is not broken and that the actor feels completely safe. I recommend that the surrounding actors talk to and encourage the central actor. Remind the central actor to relax. Praise him for doing a good job. Do not allow one actor to support the central actor alone. Teamwork is essential, especially with larger or heavier actors. Insist on a supportive atmosphere. Humorous comments will destroy the trust, and the exercise will become counterproductive.

► *Trust Run*
(Group Exercise)

Have the actors assemble in a large, open area. One actor stands in the center, while the other actors move back to create a circle in which they are approximately six feet apart. With eyes closed, the central actor runs in whatever direction he chooses. The other actors catch the running actor, gently slowing him to a stop, turning him around, and sending him off in another direction to be again supported by the surrounding actors. After the central actor has run a few times, switch actors. Make sure the area inside the circle is free of obstacles that could create a misstep or cause the central actor to lose concentration.

DISCUSSION

The Trust Run works well with large groups of fifteen or more. Take care to ensure the central actor's safety. If the other actors stop the central actor abruptly or hurt the actor in any way, the exercise will be worthless. Demand the utmost respect for the safety of the central actor during the exercise. Remind the other actors that eventually they will become the person in the middle and will want the same consideration. After the exercise, encourage the actors to talk about the feelings they had as they were running headlong into darkness.

▶ *Trust Fall*
(8 Actors—Advanced)

Have one actor stand on a chair or ladder. Six other actors stand behind this actor in two rows of three, facing each other and holding on to the wrists of the actor opposite. The remaining actor "foots" the chair or ladder so it will not move. The elevated actor then falls backward and is caught by the other actors.

DISCUSSION

This is an advanced exercise because of the potential danger involved. You and the actors must be confident that all participants are physically and mentally ready to commit to this exercise. Not only can the falling actor be hurt if not caught properly, but the other actors risk injury from the weight on their arms and back. You may want to start out with the actor standing on the floor and falling backward, then increase the height of the fall. Allow any actor who feels uncomfortable doing the exercise to sit out. The objective of this exercise is to develop trust, not to show how brave or foolhardy someone can be. Try this exercise if you feel that it offers your advanced students a chance to challenge their commitment to trust in the ensemble.

▶ Blind Walk
(Group Exercise in Pairs)

Have the class work in pairs. One actor wears a blindfold; the other actor leads the blindfolded actor about the classroom and outside if possible. The leader may not touch the actor being led: guiding must be accomplished by using vocal directions. Encourage the blindfolded actor to use the senses of smell, touch, taste, and hearing to explore the environment. After ten minutes, have the actors switch roles.

DISCUSSION

For the Blind Walk, I recommend side coaching. Have the actors note the changes in the ground as they move from sidewalk to grass, how sounds intensify, and how distances seem altered. Remind them to listen to and trust their partner's instructions. Have them touch trees, chairs, and rocks. Have them smell flowers, leaves, someone's perfume. Ask them to taste water from the water fountain. To prepare for this exercise, bring in diced pieces of apple, sour candies, and salted nuts so the actors can further explore the sense of taste.

If actors are having trouble with the Blind Walk, I let the leader hold the blindfolded actor's hand. This lets the blindfolded actor know he has not been abandoned and creates an immediate bond between the partners.

▶ *Head Holding*
(Group Exercise in Pairs)

Have one actor in each pair lie face up on the floor. The second actor sits behind the reclining actor and cradles his head in her hands. With fingers entwined and thumbs running down either side of the back of Actor 1's neck, Actor 2 supports the head and slowly massages the neck with the thumbs. Actor 2 gently raises Actor 1's head off the floor, rotates it from side to side, and moves it forward, back, left, right, and around in small circles, massaging the neck the entire time. After five minutes, have the partners switch roles.

DISCUSSION

Before beginning this exercise, make sure no one has a neck injury. If someone does, have that actor participate only in giving the massage. Side coach the class throughout the exercise, reminding the massaging actors to be gentle and not to move their partner's head too quickly. The objective of the exercise is for the reclining actor to relax and relinquish control of the head.

▶ *Face Touch*
(Group Exercise in Pairs)

First, have the actors wash their hands. Then, sitting cross-legged facing each other, the actors decide who is Actor 1 and who is Actor 2. Actor 1 closes his eyes and Actor 2 gently explores Actor 1's face with her fingers, touching the jaw, nose, hairline, eyelids, lips, and other features. Also have Actor 2 visually examine Actor 1's face, noting the different textures, lines, colors. After a few minutes, have the partners switch roles.

DISCUSSION

People are very protective of their head and very sensitive to having their face touched, so make sure the actors are ready to accept the trust and intimacy required for Head Holding and Face Touch. I have discovered that these exercises work best when the partners are either male and female or female and female. Many men feel more comfortable working with a female partner. Don't press the issue, but remind the actors that they need to become comfortable working with *everyone*, including persons of the same gender.

▶ *Obstacle Course*
(2 Actors)

Set up a simple yet challenging obstacle course using chairs, boards, tables, boxes, and similar objects. Actor 1 is blindfolded and Actor 2 tries to guide Actor 1 through the course. Actor 1 can ask questions but must rely only on Actor 2's verbal directions. If the blindfolded actor touches *any* of the obstacles, the team's turn is over. Add to the challenge by designing the course so the blindfolded actor not only walks but must crawl, step, and wiggle through the maze. For example, have Actor 1 crawl under a board suspended between two chairs, step into a circle of plastic cups half filled with water, or leap through a flaming hoop. (Just joking about that last one, but you get the idea.) At the end of the course, position an object, such as an eraser, that the blindfolded actor can pick up to end the exercise.

DISCUSSION

With each new team, change the configuration of the obstacle course slightly so that no one can memorize the layout. Emphasize not only the trust factor in the exercise, but also the listening and communication skills needed to complete the course.

Although the trust exercises create perceived dangers, in reality there is little chance of bodily harm. No one falls very far in the Trust Circle, no one runs out into a busy street in the Trust Run, and no one is permanently maimed by negotiating the Obstacle Course. However, the perceived danger does require an actor to relinquish power to the other actors and trust in them.

It will take time to develop both personal and ensemble trust. These exercises are just the beginning. As the actors get to know one another's strengths and weaknesses, remind them that it is through discipline and teamwork that they become stronger. Competition within the ensemble should be discouraged. *Process* is more important than *product* in a workshop.

IMPORTANT

Because no one knows what will happen from one moment to the next in an improvised scene, remind your actors about the need for physical control onstage. Many actors become very physical during the scenes and exercises. Even though physicality may be a valid choice for the character or situation, there is always the danger that someone will get hurt. Violence has a way of escalating very quickly. Remind the actors that the dramatic moment of a scene usually occurs *before* the violence breaks out and that *why* the characters want to fight is much more interesting than the fight itself.

All stage combat must be choreographed and rehearsed. Improvised stage combat is dangerous. Strive to keep physical violence to a minimum because once an actor is hurt, trust may be permanently lost.

5 Working Together as an Ensemble

In improvisation, if the actors are not working together, they are working against one another. Actors who showboat, steal focus, and go for cheap laughs do a disservice to the actors who are trying to create a well-developed improvised scene. Ensemble work means really listening to the other actors and exercising give-and-take onstage. It requires individual actors to relinquish power and to trust that their partners will make workable choices. This can be extremely difficult for actors who think they always know the right way to do an exercise or the best choice in a scene. The nature of improvisation dictates that there is no single correct choice. Many choices are valid, and even a choice that seems counterproductive to the scene can be saved if the actors are working as a team.

Like trust, an ensemble spirit takes time to develop. As an actor, give yourself time to establish a mental and physical link with the ensemble. Even when not participating in an exercise, notice how the other actors' minds are working, the choices they are making, and the way they are adapting to the evolving scene. This, too, helps create an ensemble spirit. The more you understand your partners' ways of working (whether in an improv or a written scene), the better your chances of working together effectively.

▶ Halftime Show
(Group Exercise)

Have the actors, without speaking or using their hands to give directions, move together to form a giant letter, like a marching band in a football halftime show. They can spell out a word or random letters. Remind the actors to be aware of one another's placement and adapt to the changes.

▶ Rabbit/Duck/Elephant
(Group Exercise)

Have the actors stand in a circle. Position yourself in the center of the circle, point to an actor, and say the word *rabbit, duck,* or *elephant.* It takes three actors to "create" an animal. Depending on the animal you've selected, the actor to whom you've pointed must display the buck teeth of the rabbit (using the fingers), the bill of a duck (using the hands), or the trunk of the elephant (using an arm). At the same time the actors on either side must provide bunny ears (one each), webbed feet (a right and left hand splayed and projected at the middle actor's waist), or elephant ears (again, one each). The three actors must complete their animal before you count to three. Whoever does the wrong animal part or doesn't do it in the allotted time stands in the center and chooses the next actor and animal.

DISCUSSION

This is a fun, silly exercise that enhances working together. Feel free to add other animals to the exercise and make up appropriate three-person movements. For example, have the middle actor become a beaver by making buck teeth with his fingers. The side actors then paddle the middle actor's butt. Or have the middle actor become a dog by panting and barking while one of the side actors lifts a leg. You get the idea.

▶ Counting
(Group Exercise)

Have the actors join you in standing in a circle. Show an action to the actor on your left and say one. That actor must then turn to the left, repeat or mirror the original action, and say two—with the same inflection you used when you said one. That actor then repeats the action for the next actor on the left and says three; the process continues around the circle. Remind the actors to repeat the action and the vocal inflection exactly.

DISCUSSION

Counting is a physical version of the children's game of telephone. Obviously, there will be mistakes, and these will make the exercise more interesting. Expect wrong numbers, wrong movements, and lots of laughter. Don't encourage these things, just try to keep each actor focused on mirroring the preceding actor. Remind the group that anything given must be passed along. If someone laughs and corrects a number, the next person must laugh and correct the number the same way.

▶ Mirror
(Group Exercise in Pairs)

Have each pair of actors stand face to face and decide who will be Actor 1, who Actor 2. Actor 1 is the leader. Actor 2 is Actor 1's reflection. Slowly, Actor 1 begins to move, and Actor 2 must mirror Actor 1's movements. Neither should watch the other's body. Instead, they should maintain eye contact at all times. Once the actors seem to be working in unison, have Actor 2 become the leader and Actor 1 the reflection.

DISCUSSION

Mirror is a staple of acting classes. I recommend side coaching in this exercise. Remind the actors to concentrate, work together, and as the leader, not to try to fool the other actor with quick movements. Eye contact is very important. Get the actors to work together physically. Remind the mirror actors to attempt to mirror their partner's facial movements as well.

► *Changing Mirror*
(Group Exercise in Pairs)

After all the actors have had a chance to lead the Mirror exercise, have them find new partners. Again, one will lead and the other will reflect. This time, whenever you say change, leadership must pass from one actor to the other without breaking the rhythm of the movements. Have the actors switch from leader to reflection and back again many times. Remind the actors that this transition should be smooth and imperceptible. An observer should not be able to tell who is the leader and who is the reflection.

► *Vocal Mirror*
(Group Exercise in Pairs)

Have the actors do the Mirror exercise, but in addition to performing the physical reflection, have them also do a vocal reflection by speaking at the same time and saying the same thing. Have the actors go slowly at first, and caution them not to get so caught up in the verbal that they forget to mirror the physical. When they switch leadership, the "story" should continue uninterrupted.

DISCUSSION

Vocal Mirror is wonderful for getting actors to work and think together. Have each actor pair with many different partners to see with whom they feel most in sync.

 ## Listening Argument
(Group Exercise in Pairs)

Have each pair of actors decide on a topic about which to disagree. This can be as simple as what movie to see or as important as a difference in religious views. Now have both actors talk at the same time, arguing yet listening to and using their arguments against each other.

DISCUSSION

Side coaching can be useful during Listening Argument. Outshouting a partner is not the objective of this exercise; outthinking and outlistening are. Keep both actors arguing and using their words against each other.

Twins
(3 Actors)

Create an interview situation. One actor acts as the host, the other two as guests. The guests must answer the host's questions at the same time, saying the same thing. The guests may find that looking into each other's eyes when answering will help them develop a "twin connection."

DISCUSSION

I recommend Twins for actors who have worked on Changing Mirror and Vocal Mirror. As an actor trying this exercise, take your time and try not to preconceive what your partner is going to say. Work at trying to connect mentally.

▶ One-Word Story
(Group Exercise)

Have the actors stand in a circle. Provide a subject and ask the group to create a story. In succession, each actor must contribute

one

word

at

a

time

until the story is completed. Tell the actors to indicate punctuation by vocal inflection and not to use run-on sentences.

DISCUSSION

Remind the actors that a good story must have a conflict and a beginning, a middle, and an end. If the actors are floundering in their attempt to create original stories, have them tell a familiar story such as *The Three Bears* or *Little Red Riding Hood*. That way, they'll already have a beginning, a middle, and an end from which to work.

▶ One-Word Interview
(4 Actors)

Have one actor play a talk-show host and ask the remaining actors to play a single interviewee. When the host asks the interviewee a question, all three actors must participate in giving the answer, each supplying one word at a time. The response may circle around the three actors as many times as it takes to answer the question.

VARIATION

Have three actors play the talk-show host and the remaining actor play a guest. In posing questions, each "host" actor may contribute only one word at a time.

▶ One-Word History
(3 or More Actors)

Give the actors an object and ask them to tell the history of that object. For example, handing them a telephone may prompt a story about Alexander Graham Bell. Giving them a pencil may elicit the history of the gigantic pencil farms of Australia. Truth is not important here, working together and mental agility are.

▶ Continuing Story
(Group Exercise)

Arrange the actors like a choir. Announce a subject and then, behaving as a musical conductor would, point to an actor to begin talking about the subject. When you give the cutoff signal, that actor must stop—mid-sentence, mid-word, mid-sound. The next actor you point to must pick up the sentence *exactly* where the previous person left off. If he doesn't pick it up exactly, or if he repeats any of what was previously said, the exercise starts over with a new subject.

DISCUSSION

The challenge of Continuing Story is to keep a story going with no break in continuity. Make sure the actors stop speaking as soon as they are given the cutoff signal.

▶ *Continuing Styles*
(Group Exercise)

Continuing Styles is the same as Continuing Story except that the story must be told in a certain style or genre—a detective story, a romance novel, a science-fiction book, a children's book (to make it really difficult, ask for the work of a specific author, like Dr. Seuss), a biology textbook, a *Cosmopolitan* article, or the back of a cereal box.

DISCUSSION

Have the actors stay true to the style of the story. If they are unfamiliar with the genre, have them read a romance novel, or the back of a Froot Loops box, or a VCR instruction booklet. The more knowledgeable an improvisational actor becomes, the more interesting the scenes she is in will be.

▶ *Group Roll*
(Group Exercise)

Have all the actors in the class lie face up, shoulder-to-shoulder, in a row on the floor. Place a pillow or similar light-weight, nondangerous object on the stomach of the actor at one end. As a group, the actors must roll together in order to move the object from that end of the row to the other without using their hands.

▶ *Group Mime*
(Group Exercise)

Have the actors work as a team to accomplish a mimed task. Emphasize the need to watch one another and to be aware of what is being established.

EXAMPLES

- Pick up a gigantic rock.
- Flip a huge tortilla.
- Turn a schoolyard merry-go-round.
- Make a clay reproduction of the Statue of Liberty.

▶ Changing Ball Toss
(Group Exercise)

Have the actors form a circle and begin to throw an imaginary tennis ball among themselves. As the actors become comfortable dealing with the mimed ball's size, weight, and speed, change the type of ball being thrown (baseball, basketball, billiard ball, ping pong ball, bowling ball, etc.).

DISCUSSION

Use side coaching during Changing Ball Toss. Remind the actors to make the ball seem real and to be sensitive to changes in size, weight, and speed as the type of ball changes.

▶ Charades
(2 Teams)

Divide the class in half. Writes titles of books, films, TV shows, old sayings, quotes from Shakespeare, etc., on slips of paper and drop them in a container. Each member of a team selects one slip of paper and nonverbally acts out for the remaining team members what is written on it. Time each person. The team guessing the answers in the least time overall is the winner. Limit the time to three minutes per clue and alternate turns between teams. Standard charade clues may be used—for example, opening the hands for a book title, breaking down the syllables on the arm, and touching the nose to let the team know it got the correct answer.

DISCUSSION

This age-old parlor game requires quick thinking. Side coaching can be valuable. If a team is not understanding an actor's clues, encourage the actor to move quickly to another choice.

▶ *Diamond Follow-the-Leader*
(Group Exercise)

Have the actors stand in a diamond formation and face one corner. The actor in this corner is the leader, and the rest of the class must follow his movements. (This exercise is the same as follow-the-leader except the actors remain stationary, in the diamond formation.) If the leader turns to the left, he transfers leadership to the actor at the point of the left corner. A turn to the right gives the leadership to the person at the point of the right corner. If the actor turns around (one hundred and eighty degrees), the leadership goes to the person at the point of the opposite corner.

DISCUSSION

As leadership passes from one corner to the next, make sure the transition is smooth. Remind the leader to begin slowly, that the exercise is follow-the-leader, not confuse-the-followers.

▶ *Who's the Leader?*
(Group Exercise)

Have one actor stand in the center of a circle with her eyes closed while you quietly designate one of the actors in the circle to be the leader. The central actor then opens her eyes, and everyone in the circle plays follow-the-leader, trying not to give away the leader's identity. When the central actor discovers the leader (or selects the wrong person) the exercise is over. Repeat the exercise using a different central actor and a different leader.

▶ Machines
(Group Exercise)

Have one actor go onstage and begin performing a simple repetitive action while making a corresponding nonsense sound. A second actor becomes another part of the same "machine" by joining the first actor onstage and creating another action/sound. The process continues until all the actors have joined together to build an interesting machine.

DISCUSSION

Machines run properly only if all their parts are working in harmony. Remind the actors that variety is interesting and encourage them to use different levels, sounds, and movements so they won't end up with a boring machine. Side coach and have the machine speed up, slow down, run amok, or break down.

VARIATION 1

Have the actors recreate a real machine—a vacuum cleaner, a blender, a computer, a carwash, etcetera.

VARIATION 2

Have the actors create a machine based on a concept or a word—a "blue" machine, a "love" machine, a "god" machine, a "Bob" machine. Encourage three-dimensional thinking. For example, to depict a blue machine, one actor might blow his nose, another might blow bubbles, another might caress her blue jeans, another might act depressed, and still another might sing the blues. As long as the actors interconnect as a machine, anything goes.

▶ *Model/Artist/Clay*
(Group Exercise in Threes)

Divide the class into groups of three. Each group decides who is the model, the artist, and the clay. The clay faces the artist with her back to the model. The model strikes a pose, and the artist must use gestures—without touching or speaking—to mold the clay into the pose the model has assumed.

DISCUSSION

Model/Artist/Clay encourages observation and teamwork. It is essential that the artists mold or guide the clay by gesture, not by assuming the pose themselves.

▶ *Energy Circle*
(Group Exercise)

Have the actors stand with you in a circle and join hands. With your eyes closed, gently squeeze the hand of the person on your left. That person allows the energy of that "pulse" to go through the arm, across the shoulders, and down the other arm and then gently passes the squeeze on to the next actor, who also passes it on. Slowly increase the speed of the pulse until it is racing around the circle. Try sending the pulse in the opposite direction. Experiment with sending more than one pulse. Eventually, try sending a pulse in both directions and see if the actors can keep the energy and concentration going in the correct direction.

DISCUSSION

It sometimes helps to have the actors visualize the pulse as energy or electricity. Have them concentrate on reacting quickly and on squeezing with only one hand, not both.

▶ *Supernova*
(Group Exercise)

Have the actors stand with their eyes closed, arms at their sides and feet shoulder width apart. Each should imagine that his or her solar plexus contains an "energy marble" that emits a powerful light and should choose a color for the light. Then *slowly* talk the actors through the exercise.

Begin by having them imagine the energy/light filling the stomach and slowly radiating into the chest, hips, shoulders, thighs, upper arms, back, knees, forearms, calves, neck, face, feet, hands, fingers, and toes. Have them feel the energy/light filling their bodies. Ask them to imagine the light growing in intensity and shooting out of their fingers, toes, and the top of their head. Have them imagine their body is illuminated like a light bulb, filling the room with their own personal light. (Have the actors lift their arms if they wish to help send the energy/light out.) Then have them push the energy/light out beyond the room and the building until it covers the city, the state, the country, and the oceans.

Have them imagine the energy/light expanding until it covers the earth. Then have them send it out toward the moon, the sun, and the rest of the universe. Have them visualize themselves as a powerful beacon with the middle of their body the source of the energy. To end the exercise, simply have the actors open their eyes.

DISCUSSION

This is an uplifting and empowering visualization exercise. Most actors feel powerful and focused after doing it. I recommend this exercise to all actors who feel the need to energize prior to doing an audition or performance, or who merely want to center themselves physically and mentally.

► *Hand-Clap Circle*
(Group Exercise)

Have the actors stand with you in a circle. Each actor puts the palm of the left hand under the right hand of the person on the left. The right hand will be on the palm of the person on the right. With your right hand, clap the left palm of the actor to your right, as quickly as possible. Each actor repeats and continues the clap around the circle in a domino effect. Once the hand-clap can move around the circle at a fast pace, change hand positions and direction.

Trust and an ensemble spirit don't develop overnight. If you continue using these exercises, your actors will gradually discover that the support of the ensemble will make them more confident and creative and that their needs and those of the ensemble are one and the same.

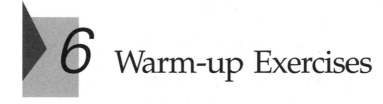

6 Warm-up Exercises

Warming up is essential for an actor. Physical and vocal warm-ups are almost universally practiced. But mental warm-ups, despite being the most important, are the least practiced. A focused, flexible, quick mind is the most vital tool of the creative actor.

Some of the exercises in this chapter are intended to improve mental/physical/vocal coordination. Some require concentrating on making sure specific tasks are accomplished or blocked out. Still others will help speed up the thought processes. Rarely does an exercise work only on one level. Even an exercise as simple as Simon Sez involves concentration, listening, reacting, and physical coordination.

Use these warm-up exercises at the beginning of each class to get the mental juices flowing. Start out slowly and build speed as the actors' ability increases. Emphasize quick thinking, mental agility, spontaneity, and three-dimensional thinking.

▶ (The ever popular) Oooh-Aaah
(Group Exercise)

Have the actors stand in a circle, then "throw" a physical action and a nonsense sound to one of the actors in the circle. That actor must "return" the same action and sound back to you, then immediately throw a new action and sound to another actor in the circle. That actor returns the new action and sound, then throws a different action and sound to a different actor. This continues until an actor fails to return the action/sound to the original actor, takes too long to respond, preconceives an action, or makes some other mistake. Mistakes *will* happen. When they do, the errant actor restarts the exercise by creating a new action/sound and throwing it to another actor. Have the actors get used to beginning again immediately and not dwelling on "failures." Emphasize how important it is for the actors to maintain eye contact. Eye contact creates a connection so the actors know to whom the action/sound is being thrown.

Once the actors understand the basic idea of the exercise, have everyone stomp their feet and yell before beginning the exercise and when someone makes a mistake. The stomping and yelling stops as soon as an action/sound is thrown. This increases the energy level and gets everyone moving.

DISCUSSION

This reaction exercise gives the actors the inalienable right to make fools of themselves. Let the actors know this, as it's important that they allow themselves the freedom to be spontaneous and not preconceive. This is a wonderful way to get the actors' energies flowing and to avoid their tendency to try to be clever. Ask them not to think in this exercise, just to react.

 ## Name Six
(Group Exercise)

Have the actors stand in a circle and quickly pass around a chalkboard eraser, rolled newspaper, hair brush, or similar object. Stand in the center with your eyes closed so you can't see who has the object. Then yell stop. Whoever has the object is "it," and must name six items in a category you supply. ("Name six states east of the Mississippi River.") The actor who is "it" passes the object on and must name at least six such items before the object makes a complete circle. If the actor succeeds, she gets to be in the center and give the next category. If the actor doesn't succeed, the exercise is repeated with the same person in the center, but with a new category.

DISCUSSION

Name Six allows the "non-it" players to observe how other actors deal with performance. The actors who are "it" must try to block out the advancing object (the time limit) and concentrate on the task of naming the six items. What often happens is that they begin jumping around, censoring their answers, and panicking as the passed object gets closer and closer. Remind the actors to relax, focus, and concentrate even while trying to think quickly in a short amount of time.

Increase or decrease the number of answers in a category depending on the number of students in the class. Make sure the categories are challenging, but neither impossible nor too easy.

GOOD EXAMPLES

- Name six films with one-word titles.
- Name six breeds of dogs.
- Name six dry cereals.
- Name six singing duos.
- Name six herbs.
- Name six sports that don't require a ball.

- Name six colors.
- Name six thirteenth-century women poets.

▶ *Name Six Plus*
(Group Exercise)

This is the same exercise as Name Six. However, after the "it" actor has a go at the category, point randomly to other actors in the circle and ask each to come up with another example of the category. This keeps the other actors on their toes because they never know when they may be called upon.

▶ *Hot Subject*
(Group Exercise)

For this variation of the game of hot potato, have the actors stand in a circle. Choose a broad subject category and toss a chalkboard eraser or other nonlethal object to any actor. The actor must name as many items in that category as possible. When the actor can no longer add to the list, he throws the object to another actor in the circle, who then must continue naming items from the same category without repeating any. The exercise ends when the actor holding the object repeats an item or takes too long to respond. The actor with the object must come up with at least three items before passing it on.

Examples

- Kinds of flowers.
- Play titles.

- Types of sports in the Olympics.
- Kinds of insects.
- Cities.
- Names of candy bars.

 ## Word Association
(Group Exercise)

Have the actors stand in a circle. Ask one of the actors to begin by saying any word that comes to mind. The next actor says the first word that this word triggers in his mind. The third actor must respond only to the immediately preceding word, not to the word said by the first actor. For example, the first actor says *marriage,* and the second says *rocks.* If the third actor says *pebbles,* there is an obvious link only to the word *rocks.* But if the third actor says *divorce,* she clearly was unable to block out the word *marriage.*

DISCUSSION

This exercise employs the psychiatric technique of free association. Emphasize the need to resist preconceiving and instead to say absolutely the first word that comes to mind. Also remind the actors they must concentrate only on the immediately preceding word.

Expert
(1 Actor)

Have an actor go onstage as an expert on a topic provided by the class. The actor must do a two-minute monologue on the subject.

VARIATION

If the actor says ah or uh during the monologue, the turn is over.

 ## Debate
(3 Actors)

Have three actors go onstage. One actor plays a moderator; the other two play experts on whatever subject is picked. One must take the pro view, the other the con. The moderator strives to keep the two experts on task. The moderator can ask for questions from the audience.

I/My Interview
(Group Exercise)

Tell one of the actors who she is or what she has done, and then have her sit center stage. The other actors are reporters sent to interview her. The reporters must raise their hands and wait for the interviewee to call on them. The interviewee must remain in character and answer all questions as completely as possible. The challenge is that the interviewee cannot say the pronouns *I* or *my*, to include contractions with *I* and the reflexive pronoun *myself*. The interviewee's turn is over when she says *I* or *my* or a two-minute time limit is reached.

Last Letter Slap-Clap-Snap
(Group Exercise)

Have the actors stand in a circle and begin a rhythm by slapping the thighs, clapping the hands, and snapping the fingers of the left, then the right hand. Once the group can sustain the rhythm, say a word on the second snap. By the second snap of the next series, the actor on your left must come up with a word that begins with the last letter of your word. For example, if you say *god*, the next actor might say *dog*. The actor on his left might say *gravy*. The next actor might say *yellow*, and so on around the circle. Words cannot be repeated, and each word must be said on the second snap.

DISCUSSION

As an interesting experiment prior to this exercise, show how easy it is to place stumbling blocks in an actor's path. Mention that you are tired of hearing the word *elephant* as a word beginning with *e*, so that word is forbidden. Without fail someone will say *elephant*. You've placed it in the actors' minds and most will be unable to remove it unless they concentrate.

VARIATION

Have the actors think of words for the second or third letter rather than the last letter. Also, when a word ends in a vowel *(a, e, i, o, u)*, reverse direction and have the person on the right come up with the new word. In this variation, the direction will change many times, requiring the players to think faster and keep alert.

▶ *Object Transformation*
(Group Exercise)

Begin by miming a simple object—a ball, for example. Bounce it, spin it on your finger, use the object as you normally would. Once the person on your left knows what the object is, pass it to that person. She must take the ball and slowly, after first maintaining an action appropriate for a ball, initiate a new action that transforms the ball into another object; she then performs only that new action. (For example, the bouncing ball can become a yo-yo simply by adjusting the movement of the arm.) The new object is then passed to the next person, who uses it until he finds an action that transforms it into something else.

DISCUSSION

It often takes time to discover a new action. Advise the actors not to panic or worry about how long it takes, but to really discover how an action can be transformed.

▶ *Simon Sez*
(Group Exercise)

Have the actors stand in a central area. Then stand on a chair so you can be seen by everyone. Tell the actors that as in the classic children's game, if they execute any action you don't preface with Simon Sez, they will be out of the game. (If you say, "Simon Sez touch your nose," they must touch their nose. If you say, "Slap your forehead," and they do, they're out.) Have the actors who are out sit on the floor where they're standing. This makes it easier to repeat the exercise.

Begin the exercise with the statement, "Simon Sez the game begins," and tell them that the rules of the exercise are in force until you say, "Simon Sez the game is over." (After you announce the game has begun, ask them to nod if they understand the rules. Some will nod. They're out.)

DISCUSSION

Warn the actors that you are the world's meanest Simon Sez player and that they will all, eventually, be out. Then go out of your way to make the actors relax and lose concentration. If they're new students ask them their names.

If they answer, they're out. Ask them if they realize they moved when you know they didn't. If they answer, they're out. Talk to them in between directives. When they are all out (and if you are doing it right, they eventually all will be), ask whether they want to try again and motion for them to stand. They'll say yes and stand. They're out.

After a few rounds, the actors will be less easily tricked, and you will see a dramatic increase in their concentration.

► *A-B-C Circle*
(Group Exercise)

Have the actors stand in a circle. Point to one actor and say the letter *a*. That actor must come up with a word that begins with *a*. Immediately, the actor to the first actor's left must also come up with a word beginning with *a*. The process continues around the circle until someone takes too long to come up with a word. At that point the direction changes and you give the new actor the next letter—*b*. The exercise continues until the class reaches the end of the alphabet or a word is repeated. If a word is repeated, the game starts over from *a*. No words from the previous games are allowed.

DISCUSSION

A-B-C Circle should move as quickly as possible. If anyone pauses or says um, quickly switch direction by pointing to the next actor and saying the next letter. This exercise encourages quick thinking and memory skills.

VARIATION

For a simpler version, move through the letters of the alphabet immediately, after only one word beginning with each letter has been given. The first actor says a word that begins with *a,* the second a word that begins with *b,* and so on until the end of the alphabet. If someone takes too long, switch direction.

▶ ## Concentration
(Group Exercise)

Have the actors stand in a circle, and number them consecutively. Begin the exercise with the clap-slap-snap pattern used in Last Letter. On the first snap the actor must say his own number, on the second snap, she must say the number of someone else in the circle. For example, Actor 6 would say six on the first snap, then another actor's number—let's say eleven—on the second snap. Actor 11 would say eleven on the first snap and another number—let's say two—on the second snap. An actor who doesn't say the numbers on the correct snaps, breaks the rhythm, or says an invalid number is out. When an actor goes out, that number is removed from the game and can't be used. It's important that you regularly announce the numbers that can still be used. To establish the rhythm of the exercise, you might begin by chanting, "Con-cen-tra-tion, Con-cen-tra-tion, keep the rhy-thm go-ing one, five"—and you're off.

DISCUSSION

The Concentration exercise encourages quick thinking and memory skills. The actors have to remember which numbers have been removed and which are still available. Speed up the tempo as the number of players dwindles.

VARIATION

Make Concentration a bit more advance by using words instead of numbers.

▶ Commercial
(1 Actor)

Have an actor go onstage and give that person a type of product to sell. The actor must create a thirty-second commercial for that product.

DISCUSSION

Steer actors away from using real product names by encouraging them to create original names. Suggest they sing (literally!) the praises of the product. Have them play multiple roles in selling the product or create a new slogan for the product. Encourage the actors to take risks!

▶ Personal Commercial
(1 Actor)

Have each actor create a thirty-second commercial about himself or herself. It can be in the form of a testimonial, a song and dance, slice of life, can employ multiple characters—anything, as long as it is in the style of a commercial and doesn't go over thirty seconds.

▶ Backtalk
(Group Exercise in Pairs)

Have the paired actors stand back to back. Without speaking, and by moving only their backs, they must convey whatever emotions or states of being you call out. Emotions include love, hate, joy, and envy. States of being include such things as drunk, cuddly, sexy, neurotic, and inspired.

▶ *What Would You Be If?*
(Group Exercise)

Have the actors stand in a circle. Choose an actor and
ask the class to think of that actor in the abstract. Ask what
the actor would be if transformed into a type of car, animal,
or fruit; a subject in school; a song title; a type of crime; a
style of dance; or anything else you can think of.

DISCUSSION

This exercise encourages abstract thinking. Insist that
the group give honest answers. Just because someone is
wearing purple doesn't mean he would necessarily be a
grape. Have the class explore what the actor might truly
turn into.

▶ *In Everyone's Life*
(1 Actor)

Have an actor go onstage, and ask that person a question that elicits a memory or an emotional response. For
example, "In everyone's life there's been a time they've been
caught in a lie. What was your lie?" The actor can either
respond truthfully or make something up, but either way
must answer immediately.

DISCUSSION

Try a variety of questions: "In everyone's life there's
been an embarrassing moment. What was your most embarrassing moment?" "In everyone's life there's been a first
love. Who was your first love?" "In everyone's life there's
been a time they did something wrong and got caught.
What did you do?"

► *Murderer*
(Group Exercise)

Have the actors sit on the floor in a circle with their eyes closed. Tap one actor on the head. This actor is the "murderer." Once the murderer is picked, the actors open their eyes and try to discover who the murderer is without being "killed." The murderer kills victims by winking at them. When winked at, a victim silently counts to three, makes a disgusting noise, and dies. If an actor in the circle thinks she knows who the murderer is, she closes her eyes and raises her hand. As soon as three actors think they know who the murderer is, ask them to identify the murderer. If they are wrong, they are permanently out of the exercise.

DISCUSSION

Because of the relative absence of movement (which should be limited to heads turning, eyes winking, and bodies dropping), Murderer encourages physical control and observation.

VARIATION

Inform the actors that there can be more than one murderer and pick multiple murderers, or make everyone a murderer (yes, murderers can be killed).

► *Family Portraits*
(Group Exercise)

Divide the class in half. One group goes center stage and creates a "family portrait" based on a type of family you announce. After three seconds, shout freeze. The actors must freeze in their portrait positions. When you call change, the first group moves offstage and the second group enters and creates its family portrait.

EXAMPLES

- A family of accountants.
- A family of fish.
- The Large Buttocks family.
- A family of weight lifters.
- A family of Elvises.
- The Dolly Parton family.
- A family of snakes.

DISCUSSION

Make the exercise fun and spontaneous. Call out ten or fifteen different families in rapid succession to get the actors moving and reacting.

▶ *This Is Not a Stick*
(Group Exercise)

Place a stick downstage center. Have each actor in turn use the stick in a way that transforms it into something else. For example, one actor might swing the stick like a baseball bat. Another might use it as a straw. Another might move it across the ground like a snake or twirl it overhead like a helicopter blade. Each new object must have some sticklike qualities (for example, you can turn the stick into a diving board but not into a swimming pool).

DISCUSSION

Use any kind of stick without splinters. (I use a three-foot piece of quarter-inch doweling.) Have each actor work with the stick five or six times during this exercise, so that the class really explores what the stick can become. Once the obvious stick transformations have been used, have the actors work with the stick in ways that will give them new ideas—waving it, rolling it, or tossing it, for example. The actions of the stick will suggest ideas for transformations.

VARIATION

Use an object other than a stick, such as a roll of toilet paper. I've seen a roll of toilet paper become a ticker tape being read, a red carpet being unrolled, a soda can, a telephone, and even the gauze being wrapped around a mummy. Try other objects, such as a trash can lid or a cardboard box.

▶ *Honey Walk*
(Group Exercise)

In a large, open space free of any obstacles, have the actors stand in a line, facing front, approximately three feet apart. Have them close their eyes and imagine that they are wearing a scuba tank, so that they can continue breathing normally during the exercise. Lead the actors on an imaginary journey as they walk *slowly* through a succession of substances—warm fog, water, vegetable oil, motor oil, honey, hardened Jell-O, and wet cement. Tell the actors they are completely submerged in each substance. End the exercise by having the cement dry around the actors; ask them to break out of their cement prison.

DISCUSSION

Side coach the actors to imagine really moving through these viscous fluids. Have them explore feeling buoyant in the water and finding it progressively difficult to move through the thickening substances. Remind them that one doesn't feel wet (or oily or sticky) when completely immersed in a substance but rather when one *gets out* of the substance.

VARIATION

Change the exercise by having the actors walk in zero gravity or participate in a slow-motion race (the *last* one to cross the finish line wins). Lead them through different temperature zones. Have them pretend to be pulled around the room by invisible wires. Have them walk and dance as if they are marionettes. Ask them to do anything that forces them to move and maintain control while dealing with imaginary physical obstacles.

► *Hunter/Hunted*
(Group Exercise)

Have the actors sit on chairs in a large circle. Ask them to close their eyes while you place a "weapon" (a pillow, a sock, or a rolled-up piece of paper) somewhere within the circle. Then select two actors by tapping them on the shoulder. These two actors are "it," and the other actors can open their eyes. With their eyes still closed, the actors who are "it" must search the interior of the circle for the weapon. Whoever finds it first is the hunter; the remaining actor becomes the hunted. The hunter's job is to tag the hunted with the weapon. The hunted's objective is to find the hunter's chair and sit in it before being tagged.

DISCUSSION

Hunter/Hunted is a listening, awareness, and tactics exercise. Have the class observe how each person handles the exercise. Some will be bold, others skittish. Some will be sly, others carefree. What happens to a person on becoming the hunter? the hunted?

Remind the actors to be careful when they are wielding the weapon. Emphasize that the hunted is to be *tagged*, not hit.

Other good warm-up exercises are One-Word Story, Continuing Story, and Continuing Styles.

7 Playwriting on Your Feet

Improvisation is playwriting on your feet. It's storytelling. Everything you find in a well-written play, scene, or story you will also find in a well-performed improvisation. Unlike scripted drama, improvisation requires the actors to choose (or discover as the scene progresses) the story's who, where, what, when, why, and how. I know this sounds like high school journalism class, but these are also the fundamental building blocks of all good theatre. In acting, we give these basic elements other names: character (who), setting (where), plot (what), time (when), motivation (why), and action (how). Breaking a scene down into these essential elements gives the actor a clear idea of how to build a scene.

As an example, let's establish a simple two-character scene that can be changed dramatically by adjusting any of the basic story elements. The premise of the improvised scene is two people on a first date.

Who/Character

- Who am I? What is my character's name? age? race? religion? sexual orientation? occupation? educational level? dialect? and so on.
- What is my relationship to the other characters in the scene?

- How does my character behave?
- What role (or roles) is my character playing?

EXAMPLES

- An elderly man and woman.
- An ex–husband and wife.
- Two members of the same sex.
- A boss and an employee.
- A Miss America and her judge.
- A stepbrother and stepsister.
- Aliens from another planet.
- Stanley Kowalski and Stella du Bois.
- Two teenagers.
- A famous person and the local librarian.
- Two six-year-olds.
- A wolf and a sheep.

When creating a character in a general category, such as a famous person and the local librarian, your boundaries are limitless. What kind of famous person? politician? local hero? rock star? television news anchor? mass murderer? What about that local librarian—an ex-porn star? an expert on quantum physics? recently released from the state mental hospital? illiterate? Choices, choices, choices.

There are two types of character work associated with improvisation. The first is creating an original character during the course of a scene. The second is putting an existing or preconceived character into different situations. As an actor in a completely improvised scene, you will create your character as you go along. If you are playing a character in a written play, you may want to improvise how that character behaves in a scene only referred to in the play.

The *roles* your character plays are also important. Your

character will act differently when confronted by his mother, hugged by his son, lectured by his boss, or seduced by his neighbor. He is always the same character, but his behavior changes with each role he assumes, whether son, father, employee, or lover.

The variations are endless, but choosing interesting characters helps make an interesting scene. Remember, all acting is relationship driven. All good stories are based on the relationships the characters have with one another. Who the characters are in relation to one another motivates the action of the scene. Also remember that any scene, no matter what kinds of characters are created, can be made either humorous or serious by how the actors perform it.

Where/Setting

- Where am I?
- Where is this scene set? on which planet or continent? in what state and city? at which address? in which room?
- Where was I immediately before this scene?
- Where am I going after this scene?
- What objects are in this setting?

EXAMPLES

- At a McDonald's in Moscow.
- Sitting in the sun at a bullfight in Toledo, Spain.
- At a Motel 6 in Tilghman County, Georgia.
- In an elevator ascending toward heaven.
- In the same elevator descending toward hell.
- On 49th Street in New York City during a blackout.

- On a porch swing in the middle of summer in Loveland, Colorado.
- Washed up on the shore of an uncharted island.
- In a jail cell in Mexico City.
- Stranded in a car in the middle of a blizzard.
- In a Paris bistro.
- In the stomach of a whale.
- On a balcony above a garden in Verona, Italy.

Where a scene takes place has a dramatic effect on that scene. A husband and wife arguing over child custody will adjust their behavior depending on whether they're doing so in a library, in a movie theatre, in their living room, or in space as they repair a satellite. The more specific you can be about where you are, the more information you have to use to develop your characters and plot. If your scene is set in a restaurant, your choice of restaurants is important. The Four Seasons has a different ambience than Pedro's Taco a Go Go does, and your characters will react differently. If your scene takes place in a stranded car, what kind of car is it? a limousine? a VW van? an armored personnel carrier? Each will take your scene in a different direction. Sometimes you will want to chose a setting that complements your scene; other times you will want to chose one that creates conflict. Where a scene takes place can also set its mood, tone, and tempo.

In addition, your *setting* undoubtedly will contain objects that you can use to help propel the scene—the food, appliances, pots, pans, and silverware in a kitchen; the towels, Magic Fingers, television, bar, mirrored ceiling, and Gideon Bible in a motel room; or the magic potions, crystal ball, and swords in a Gypsy wagon.

Never underestimate the importance of creating a strong "where" in a scene.

When/Time

- When is this scene taking place?
- What time of day?
- What day and what year?
- At what point in this character's life?

EXAMPLES

- In the year 13 B.C., 2010, 1600, 1969, 1855.
- On New Year's Eve.
- On the day John F. Kennedy was assassinated.
- After twelve years of sexual abstinence.
- On the Fourth of July.
- On the day a meteorite is scheduled to destroy the earth.
- At the beginning, middle, end, of a date.
- On Halloween.
- At 6:00 A.M.; at 9:30 P.M.; at 2:01 A.M.

When a scene takes place determines the actors' style of speech, mannerisms, maturity level, and even amount of knowledge. (If the scene takes place in 1750, the characters would have no knowledge of auto repair—unless they are time travelers.) A scene that takes place at 3 A.M. will have different dynamics than the same scene taking place at noon.

It isn't imperative that all scenes take place on Bastille Day, but characters who have a first date on a nondescript day at an unimportant time can make your scene nondescript and unimportant.

What/Plot

- What is going on?
- What is the story?
- What do I want?
- What is my objective/goal/desire in this scene?
- What is stopping me from getting what I want?
- What are the conflicts?

EXAMPLES

- One character wants to go home, the other wants the evening to go on forever.
- One character wants sex on the first date, the other wouldn't think of it.
- Both would like to have sex, but their wheelchairs won't fit through the hotel room door.
- One is embarrassingly shy, the other is embarrassingly brazen; one or the other wants to avoid a scene.
- He wants to know all about her past, she wants to hide it.
- He wants a goodnight kiss, she can't stand his breath.
- They want to go out again, but they are from different worlds (literally).
- What if . . .

A scene is driven by *what* the characters want. The more you want something, the more important it becomes, and the more the scene will develop. Once you get what you want, the conflict is over, and either your scene is over as well or you must develop another want. In most improvisations, because the plot is not stated at the beginning but unfolds as the scene progresses, it is important to know not only what you want to get from the other actor, but what the other actor wants to get from you.

Plot variations are endless, and when combined with different characters, times, and places, offer an unlimited amount of raw material upon which to build. This is one of the things that makes improvisation so exciting.

Why/Motivation

- Why am I doing this?
- What motivates my actions?
- Why are my partners doing what they are doing?

EXAMPLES

- He asked her out on a dare.
- She thought he was someone else.
- He thought she was rich.
- It was lust at first sight.
- She went out to make her husband jealous.
- It was arranged through a dating service.
- It was arranged by their parents.
- He asked him out as part of a fraternity prank.
- He hired her to be his girlfriend.

Why a character does something is one of the fundamental questions actors asks themselves. With a written script we can analyze motivation, but in improvisation we must make choices based on the information that is being created as the scene progresses. Motivation occurs spontaneously as your scenes and exercises evolve.

How/Action

- How am I going to get what I want?
- What do I need to do to get what I want?

- What actions/choices/tactics will help me get what I want?

EXAMPLES

- He buys her flowers and candy.
- She pouts and refuses to eat.
- He breaks down and cries.
- She massages his back.
- He fakes being sick.
- She kisses him.
- He throws his wedding ring into the ocean.
- She threatens him with Mace.
- He holds her cat ransom.

Whether you whine, cajole, shout, beat on the table, cry, or seduce, you must decide *how* you will go about getting what you want. Your actions, both physical and verbal, must take you closer to getting what your character wants and to creating an interesting scene.

Who? where? when? what? why? and how? are the basic questions you and your scene partners must deal with as your improvisation unfolds. A playwright has the luxury of taking the time to answer these questions, but an improvisational actor doesn't. The improvisational actor must make immediate choices and work with the choices of others.

Building a Scene

Whether you are acting in a commercial, a television show, or a two-hour play, if it is well written it will have a beginning, a middle, and an end. In the beginning there will be exposition that explains who (character), where (setting), what (plot), and when (time) and that sets up a conflict. In the middle the scene will continue to build, showing how (action) and explaining why (the character's motivation), until the play reaches a climax. At the end, there will be a resolution and conclusion. Or as some playwright is rumored to have said, In Act 1 get your character up a tree, in Act 2 throw rocks at him, in Act 3 get him down.

As an example, let's watch a thirty-second commercial. In it we see a man and a woman cuddling on the couch in front of a fireplace, a dog sitting at their feet. Behind them is a window through which we can see snow falling. This simple scene establishes who (a young couple in love) and where (in front of the fireplace in the living room) and a general when (a cold winter night). As the camera pans, we see a Christmas tree, so we now know more specifically when the scene takes place. The woman moves closer to the man and says, "Honey, why don't you take off your shoes?" The man looks worried and replies, "I think I'll keep them on for a little while." We now have a conflict. She wants him to take off his shoes, he doesn't want to. "Come on, get comfortable," she purrs. "I'm fine," he stutters, "want some more popcorn?" "Here," she says leaning forward, "let me help you." "I'll do it," he practically shouts and reluctantly removes his shoes. The climax occurs as the dog watches the man take off his shoes, gets a whiff of the odor coming from the man's feet, and, ears standing up, falls over. The conflict is resolved by a picture of the product and a voice-over explaining the virtues of OdorEaters. The scene ends with the loving couple kissing and the dog holding one of the man's shoes in his mouth.

Okay, it's not Emmy material, but this commercial has a beginning, a middle, an end, and a conflict. It illustrates the point that scene structure is relatively easy to follow and not that difficult to achieve in an improvised scene.

We have been exposed to this kind of scene structure

since childhood. Building a scene is basic storytelling. Whether it is *Little Red Riding Hood, A Streetcar Named Desire,* or a current film, we have seen, heard, or read stories that follow this pattern.

Every improvised scene is different and so is the way the scene is structured. File this information away in your brain and remember: the best improvised scenes are just stories well told.

8 Playwriting Exercises

▶ *Neutral Scenes*
(2 Actors)

In a neutral scene the actors are allowed to use written dialogue, but the script gives no information about who or where the characters are or what they are doing. Actors make these kinds of choices about the scene by how they deliver their lines and the physical actions they undertake during the scene. The scene is very short and can be easily memorized.

Make sure the actors agree about the scene's who, where, and what. Encourage them to take their time creating the characters and the environment, but don't allow them to deviate from the written dialogue.

SCENE 1

ACTOR 1: Hello.
ACTOR 2: Oh, hi.
ACTOR 1: What are you doing?
ACTOR 2: Nothing.
ACTOR 1: Really?
ACTOR 2: Yeah! What are you doing here?
ACTOR 1: Not much. Just this.
ACTOR 2: Oh.

ACTOR 1: Well, see you later.
ACTOR 2: Yeah, see you around.

SCENE 2

ACTOR 1: So what do you think?
ACTOR 2: I don't know.
ACTOR 1: What?
ACTOR 2: I said I don't know yet!
ACTOR 1: Why not?
ACTOR 2: I'm just not sure.
ACTOR 1: Come on, we don't have much time.
ACTOR 2: Just a minute!
ACTOR 1: Well?
ACTOR 2: Well, what?
ACTOR 1: What do you want to do?
ACTOR 2: How about trying this?

SCENE 3

ACTOR 1: How are you doing?
ACTOR 2: Fine.
ACTOR 1: I'm fine too.
ACTOR 2: That's nice.
ACTOR 1: Yeah, it is.
ACTOR 2: I mean it really is great, isn't it?
ACTOR 1: Sure it is.
ACTOR 2: Are you going?
ACTOR 1: Maybe. How about you?
ACTOR 2: Sure.
ACTOR 1: Great.
ACTOR 2: Yeah, great, isn't it.

► *The Bus Stop*
(2 Actors)

Establish a scene at a bus stop and tell the actors to begin improvising. As the scene progresses, interject specific changes they must incorporate into the situation.

EXAMPLES

- A husband and wife are waiting for a bus in Phoenix, Arizona. They are on vacation, but their car has broken down because the husband forgot to have it serviced before the trip. Through side coaching, inform the actors that the temperature is 85 degrees, 90 degrees, 95 degrees, and so on. Or alter the temperature in the opposite direction: it is 50 degrees and it starts to rain; it is 32 degrees and starts to snow; it is −10 degrees and stormy; the storm becomes a blizzard . . .
- A young couple on a date sit on a bench at a bus stop in a tough part of Detroit at 5 P.M., 11 P.M., 3 A.M.
- Two old friends are waiting for a bus in Miami, Florida. A bee buzzes around them. Then another. Then another. Now a swarm of bees surrounds them.

DISCUSSION

Bus Stop is a good introduction to side coaching a scene. The actors should accept your changes as they are given and respond to them without acknowledging you. This will help actors learn to make quick choices and adapt to new information. In the first two examples, as the weather or the time of day changes, the actors must decide quickly how to deal with those changes. In Example 3, if one of the characters establishes that she is allergic to bee stings, the characters must react to the bees immediately; if they don't care about the bees (if, for example, they are wearing beekeepers outfits), they still must acknowledge that bees surround them. Allow the actors to explore each change before moving on to the next one.

▶ *Six Scenes*
(2 Actors)

Establish a scene and have the actors develop it using only ten lines of improvised dialogue. Then ask them to memorize the dialogue they have improvised. Have them repeat the scene six times, each time changing one of the basic elements: who they are, where they are, when the scene takes place, why they are there, what is going on, and how they resolve the scene.

DISCUSSION

Although the dialogue will need to change somewhat as each element changes, have the actors try to remain true to the original concept of the improvised scene.

▶ *Freeze Tag*
(Group Exercise in Pairs)

Assign two actors to begin an activity (washing a car, painting a wall, etc.) as the rest of the class observes. When an observer sees them in a position that triggers an idea for a new scene, that person calls freeze. The actors onstage freeze their positions and the person who stopped the action tags one of the original actors out, assumes that actor's physical position, and uses dialogue to create a completely new scene. Both actors must justify their positions in the new scene. Have the class do this exercise several times.

EXAMPLE

One actor is lying on the floor and the other actor is giving CPR. An observer calls freeze, goes onstage, and tags the actor who is lying down. That actor leaves the stage and the new actor takes his place. If the new actor chooses to become Frankenstein's monster, the actor giving CPR might become a mad scientist. Or perhaps the actor lying down is a patient receiving an acupuncture treatment. The possibilities are endless.

 ## *Freeze*
(Group Exercise in Pairs)

Assign two actors an activity, such as climbing a mountain or walking on hot coals. At some point during the scene, call freeze. The actors must immediately create a new scene based on their positions. Freeze the actors several times.

DISCUSSION

Since each scene rarely goes on for more than a minute or two, this is a wonderful exercise to encourage fast thinking and decision making. Each time the action is stopped, both actors must quickly establish a new who, what, and where.

Three-Character Interview
(2 Actors)

Ask one actor to assume the role of a clerk conducting interviews for an employment agency; the other actor becomes a job applicant. During the scene, call change. The job applicant must exit and immediately return as a new character. After a while call change again; the job applicant must return as still another character.

DISCUSSION

Once the actor playing the job applicant has created three characters, have that actor take over the role of the interviewer. Make sure everyone in the class has the opportunity to play both roles. It's very difficult to watch other actors create characters and not think about alternative choices. Remind the actors not to use preconceived characters in this exercise, to rely on the spontaneity of the moment.

▶ Hitchhiker
(Group Exercise)

Set up four chairs as if they are seats in a car. Have one actor mime driving while another actor hitchhikes. The driver picks up the hitchhiker and must assume the hitchhiker's character, attitude, accent, energy, and mannerisms. As the scene progresses, another hitchhiker appears. The actors in the car stop to pick this hitchhiker up and both assume the new actor's characteristics. After a short scene, the process is repeated with a fourth actor. When the fifth actor appears, the driver exits, and the actors rotate into new positions in the car (the driver leaves, "shotgun" moves to driver, rear left to "shotgun," new hitchhiker sits rear right.) Continue the exercise until everyone in the class has been a hitchhiker, with the original driver being the last.

DISCUSSION

Side coach the actors to stay focused on the new hitchhiker's character, not to make assumptions about how that character behaves. Have the actors prepare for this exercise by reviewing the Mirror exercises.

▶ Age Walk
(Group Exercise)

Ask the actors to stand in a circle, then to begin walking in the same direction around the circle. As they walk, call out ages, beginning with three years old. As each new age is called, the actors must immediately become that age, adjusting the way they talk to one another, create relationships, and play. The actors continue walking as you increase the age to five, seven, ten, twelve, thirteen, fifteen, sixteen, eighteen, twenty, twenty-one, and twenty-five. After age twenty-five, continue to increase the age in five-year increments. Give the actors time to work on the physical, vocal, and emotional qualities appropriate for each age. Side coach where needed and emphasize staying as faithful as possible to a given age. Each actor should create a complete linear life. At age eighty, end the exercise by returning the actors to age three.

DISCUSSION

Age Walk is a wonderful physical and mental challenge. Discuss the physical changes that occurred, the relationships that developed, and other choices the actors made during the exercise. When did the characters have their first crush? their first drink? their first date? What jobs did they have? When did they marry? divorce? retire? Are these age-specific events? Were the characters late bloomers or early achievers? Did this exercise parallel the actors' real lives or were they completely fictitious? During the course of the exercise, arbitrarily remove two or three actors from the circle. "Killing" these actors makes the exercise more lifelike, since people are taken from our lives all the time. As this exercise tends to be noisy, write the ages on a chalkboard as you call them out so the actors can refer to them.

Returning to age three allows the exercise to end with positive energy. (Imagine how much energy the actors would have discussing this exercise if they were still thinking of themselves as eighty-year-olds!)

▶ *This Is Your Life*
(Group Exercise)

Have an actor sit on a chair center stage. This actor is the central character, although he has no preconceived idea about who he is; he begins the exercise as an empty slate. Individually, the other actors approach the central character and initiate scenes from the character's life. Each actor tags out the previous actor and begins a completely different scene. The scenes need not be chronological. The first scene may occur at the character's high school reunion, the next at his sixth birthday party; the following scene could be a divorce proceeding initiated after fifteen years of marriage, the next could take place at his bris—you get the idea. Each scene must incorporate who and where the characters are, and when in the central character's life the event is happening. An actor can interact with the main character more than once, and can appear in scenes from a number of chronological periods, but must do so as the character established in the first scene with the main character. This does not mean that an actor's *role* won't change: if an actor establishes herself as the wife of the central character in the first scene, she could subsequently be his girlfriend, mistress, fiancee, co-worker, ex-wife, sister-in-law (the same *character*, different *roles*).

As the central character's life is gradually revealed

through successive scenes, the actor playing the central character can add new information to each subsequent scene.

DISCUSSION

This Is Your Life not only helps to build a well-rounded character but also enhances an actor's ability to give and take, accept information, tell a story, and think in a non-linear fashion (important when working in films, which are invariably shot out of sequence). Urge the actors to create distinctly different lives for each actor playing the central character.

▶ *Where Are We?*
(Group Exercise)

Ask an actor to go onstage and by using only mimed actions and objects show where she is. When the class identifies the setting, ask other actors to go onstage and help the first actor reenforce the where by making it more specific. Encourage as many actors as possible to participate as long as they support the where.

EXAMPLE

The first actor might mime scanning groceries at a checkout counter. Other actors might then become a bagger, a customer in line, a stock clerk, shoppers pushing carts, and a person standing by the front door panhandling, each helping to reinforce the where.

DISCUSSION

Encourage the actors to relate to one another. The more specific the actors are in their mime work, the more easily the setting will become established.

Try incorporating dialogue into this exercise, but caution the actors that they may not specifically refer to where they are.

 ## *Where Were You?*
(1 Actor)

Have an actor go onstage and through mime establish where he has just come from and where he is now.

 ## *Where Are You Going?*
(1 Actor)

Have an actor begin onstage and through mime establish where she is and also where she is going when she exits.

Where Were You?/Where Are You Going?
(2 Actors)

Ask two actors to enter the stage and show where they were, where they are, and where they are going. They can do this both through action and dialogue.

DISCUSSION

Where Were You?, Where Are You Going?, and Where Were You?/Where Are You Going? help actors learn to establish a fully developed where. Characters enter a stage *from somewhere* and will *go somewhere* when they exit, and it is important that actors be able to communicate a character's connection to the larger world.

▶ *Constant Action*
(2 Actors)

Establish a scene that requires constant action or activity. The actors *must* continue talking during the exercise.

EXAMPLES

- Bailing water out of a boat.
- Eating a seven-course meal.
- Giving a dog a bath.
- Operating on a patient.
- Changing a dirty diaper.

▶ *Beginning/Middle/End*
(6 Actors)

Have two actors establish a scene's who, what, and where and begin the scene. After this beginning information has been established, call change and have two other actors assume the previous actors' characters and physical positions, continue the scene, and contribute a middle to the scene. Then call change again and have a third pair of actors bring the scene to a conclusion.

DISCUSSION

In this exercise—as in a three-act play—the beginning scene should give information, establish character, and create conflict; the middle scene should advance the action; and the final scene should provide the climax, resolution, and conclusion. Beginning/Middle/End also requires the actors to concentrate on mirroring the first pair of actors' characters, both physically and vocally. During this exercise, three different pairs of actors are playing the same characters.

VARIATIONS

Change the order to End/Middle/Beginning, Middle/End/Beginning, and so on. Like This Is Your Life, this is excellent preparation for film acting, where scenes are routinely shot out of sequence.

▶ *Past/Present/Future*
(6 Actors)

Establish a scene and have the first pair of actors play the scene as if it is in the past (how far in the past is the actors' choice). After the scene develops, call change and have the second pair of actors play the same characters in the present. Repeat the process for the third pair, who must play the same characters in the future.

DISCUSSION

Have the actors experiment with the time differences. The past scene could be the day before the present scene or any other time as long as it is *before*. Similarly, the future scene can take place three minutes or thirty years in the future or any time in between. This exercise goes hand in hand with Beginning/Middle/End.

▶ *Before and After*
(2 Actors)

Divide the class into pairs. Give each pair of actors a single photocopied page from a play and assign their roles. Ask them to improvise a scene that happens before the written scene, move seamlessly into the script, and then proceed to an improvised ending.

DISCUSSION

Ideally, the actors should be unfamiliar with the play from which their scene is taken, so that their improvised scenes are completely original. The actors should try to re-create the tone of the scene and the style of the dialogue and shouldn't negate any information given in the single page of script. When the exercise is done well, the transitions between the written and improvised material should be indiscernible.

▶ *Costume Pieces*
(2 Actors)

Assemble a wide assortment of costume pieces, such as hats, cloaks, jackets, wigs, dresses, bras, suits of armor, and false beards. Establish a scene and have each actor choose a costume as the basis for his or her character.

DISCUSSION

At times, a costume makes the character. Have the actors explore how the different costume pieces make them change physically and emotionally, and how a costume can be a springboard to interesting character choices.

VARIATION

Assign or have other members of the class assign a costume to each actor. The actor must then create a character based on this costume.

▶ *Three Objects*
(2 Actors)

Establish a scene and have the actors "find" in this environment at least three different mimed objects they can use in the scene.

DISCUSSION

Discovering mimed objects in your environment can lead to inventive improvising, since you alone determine what you find. In one memorable improvised robbery scene, the robber had a knife so the victimized businessman pulled out a gun. The robber reached into his jacket and pulled out a hand grenade, and the victim pulled a bazooka out of his briefcase. When the robber opened his jacket and announced he was wearing forty-five pounds of plastic explosives, the victim pulled out a mimed vial of "Plutonium 5000, the world's most powerful explosive"! At that point the robber decided to give up, but not before the businessman took the robber's wallet.

▶ *Family Reunion*
(Group Exercise)

Have the actors create characters who are attending a family reunion. Two actors begin the scene, which takes place in the kitchen of the home where the reunion is being held. When a third actor enters, one of the initial characters must find a reason to leave. The two remaining actors continue the scene until another actor enters, at which time one of the former twosome must find a reason to leave. Actors may enter the kitchen as many times as they want, as long as they remain the same character throughout the exercise.

Allow the actors to change characters when they reenter the scene.

▶ *Family Vacation*
(4 Actors)

Set up four chairs as if they are car seats and establish a vacation destination. The actors assume the roles of a man and wife and their two children (or any other family members they choose) beginning a vacation. The scene begins as they are leaving the house, continues with their arrival at the vacation spot, and ends when they return home.

VARIATION
(5 or More Actors)

Allow other characters to enter the scene—a park ranger, a gas station attendant, a disgruntled Disneyland employee, etcetera.

▶ *First Line/Last Line*
(2 Actors)

Decide on a line of dialogue with which to begin a scene and a line of dialogue with which to end the scene. Have the actors develop a scene between these two lines that include who, what, where, when, why, and how. The scene is over when the last line is given.

DISCUSSION

The first few times the actors attempt First Line/Last Line, write the lines of dialogue on a chalkboard or large piece of paper. Otherwise the scene may turn into "Two Actors Trying to Remember the Last Line."

► *Set the Mood*
(2 Actors)

Establish the characters and setting for a scene. Have two actors begin the scene and, without speaking, set the scene's tone or mood.

► *Sixty-Second Movie*
(Group Individual Exercise)

Allow each actor ten minutes in which to condense a movie into a sixty-second scene. The scene must tell the story and have a beginning, a middle, and an end.

DISCUSSION

Sixty-Second Movie gives actors practice in condensing plot and playing multiple characters. Time the actors, and give them a ten-second warning before time runs out.

► *Specifics*
(2 Actors)

Establish a scene. Tell the actors they can speak only in specifics. There can be no generic observations.

GENERIC CHOICE

ACTOR 1: Hey, nice dog.
ACTOR 2: Thanks.

BETTER CHOICE

ACTOR 1: Hey, isn't that an Australian dingo you have there?
ACTOR 2: Why yes it is! I use him to track down wallabies. I find it amazing that dingos are the only nonpouched carnivores native to that island continent. I call him Wilber, after my Uncle Wilber, who was killed in a prune-pitting accident in Gilroy, California, during the Garlic Festival of '69.

DISCUSSION

Specifics is a good exercise for taking things to the extreme. The more specific the better.

▶ Moment of Crisis
(2 Actors)

Establish a crisis and have the actors begin their scene at the exact moment the crisis occurs.

EXAMPLES

- The moment of impact in an auto accident.
- Being told about a death.
- Finding your spouse in bed with another person.

DISCUSSION

Moment of Crisis can help the actor find and create a scene's climax or turning point. Make sure the actors begin the scene at the peak emotional level of the crisis.

▶ Storytelling
(Group Exercise)

Ask an actor to assume the role of a storyteller and to make up a story. As the storyteller creates the story's characters (they might be trees, tables, houses, trolls, queens, frogs, magic weasels, and so on), the rest of the actors portray them onstage. The storyteller must create a complete story with a beginning, a middle, and an end.

DISCUSSION

The storyteller should allow the characters in the story an opportunity to speak so that they have a chance to further the story. The best stories permit strong give-and-take between the characters and the storyteller.

▶ Storytelling with Sound Effects
(Group Exercise)

Have the actors do the Storytelling exercise, but add a "sound supervisor" who sits next to the storyteller and contributes appropriate sound effects to enhance the story.

▶ Tag-Team Storytellers
(Group Exercise)

Have the actors do the Storytelling exercise, but designate three storytellers. One storyteller creates the beginning of the story, then passes it to the second storyteller, who creates the middle. The third storyteller ends the story. Emphasize that there must be smooth transitions from one part of the story to the next and that previously established information must not be negated.

 *9* Beginning Exercises

 *Mormon Tabernacle Freeze*
(Group Exercise)

Ask an actor to go onstage and begin an action. One of the other actors calls freeze when the first actor is in an interesting position. The actor onstage freezes in whatever position she is in, and the second actor goes onstage and creates a two-person scene with the first actor. Once the scene develops, a third actor calls freeze and goes up to create a three-person scene. One at a time, the remaining class members join the actors onstage in this same manner until everyone in the class is onstage for the final scene.

DISCUSSION

As in the Freeze and Freeze Tag exercises, the actors must justify the positions that they assume. The challenge here is to develop scenes that incorporate more and more people.

VARIATION

Have the actors do the exercise in reverse, beginning with everyone onstage. The actors leave one at a time, by saying freeze, beginning a new scene, and then finding a way to exit.

► *Whisper/Normal/Shout*
(2 Actors)

Establish a scene. Have the actors improvise, whispering the dialogue. Then have them repeat the same scene in normal voices. Finally, have them repeat the scene again, this time shouting the dialogue.

DISCUSSION

Did the change in volume change the scene? the characters? how the characters reacted? Vary the exercise by having one actor shout and the other whisper, or use some other combination of the three volume levels.

► *One Line Each*
(2 Actors)

Establish a scene. Have the actors alternate lines, allowing them to speak only one sentence at a time. Each actor must wait for the other's sentence before he or she can speak again.

DISCUSSION

The actors should avoid the temptation to use run-on sentences and should not overlap each other's dialogue. This exercise emphasizes listening and give-and-take.

► *Alphabet Scene*
(2 Actors)

Establish a scene. Give the same instructions as for One Line Each, but require that the first word of the first line begin with an *a*, the first word of the second line begin with a *b*, and so on. The scene is over when the actors have completed twenty-six lines, progressing consecutively through the alphabet.

Discussion

Alphabet Scene is a combination of One Line Each and A-B-C Circle. In creating the scene, the actors must introduce a conflict and provide a beginning, a middle, and an end.

Variation

Ask three or four or more actors to do Alphabet Scene. Try mixing up the alphabet (writing the letters on a chalkboard so the actors can follow them). Or try doing the alphabet backwards.

▶ No, It's Not
(2 Actors)

Establish a scene. Tell the actors that in developing the scene they must negate or change all the information provided by their partner. Also instruct them to be very specific in their choices.

Example

ACTOR 1: Welcome to Oz!

ACTOR 2: No, it's not Oz, it's Detroit, and I wouldn't be hanging around here in that dog outfit.

ACTOR 1: This isn't a "dog outfit"! I'm a cowardly lion!

ACTOR 2: No, you're not! You look like a french poodle.

ACTOR 1: I'm neither French nor a poodle, I'm a Basque terrorist, and I have a gun!

ACTOR 2: That isn't a gun . . .

Discussion

This is a good example of how saying no and negating established information can hinder a scene. Because this exercise requires successive denials, the scene will eventually grind to a stop when the actors are no longer able to come up with alternative choices. No, It's Not is a good way to make the point that saying yes (and yes, but) keeps the scene moving forward.

▶ No Questions
(2 Actors)

Establish a scene. Tell the actors that if one of them asks a question during the scene, the scene is over.

Discussion

This may seem like a simple exercise, but it's actually very difficult. Actors constantly ask questions in scenes to get more information and to clarify the information they have. No Questions makes the actors give positive statements, further the action, add to the information, and think about their choices.

▶ Surprise Prop
(2 Actors)

Establish a scene. Tell the actors that they must develop the scene so that the climax or conclusion is brought about by the introduction of a surprise mimed prop.

Examples

- At a bachelor party the stripper doesn't show up, but someone offers to let the revelers use his inflatable love doll.

- At a biker wedding, the groom can't find the wedding ring. The bride offers him her nose ring.
- While in bed, a husband casually asks his wife how her weekly women's club meeting went. The wife gives a long description of the meeting's agenda, after which the husband pulls out the wife's diary and confronts her with the evidence of an affair.

DISCUSSION

Surprise Prop is a good exercise to help actors discover the importance of objects and props and how they can radically change the direction of a scene.

▶ Touching
(2 Actors)

Establish a scene and require that in order to speak to each other the actors must also touch each other—by putting an arm around the other's waist, shaking hands, poking the other in the chest, and so forth—and that the touching must be justified within the context of the scene. For an added challenge establish a scene that doesn't lend itself to physical contact.

EXAMPLES

- Newlyweds on their wedding night.
- A couple getting a divorce.
- Two men in a bathroom.
- Rival cheerleaders.

DISCUSSION

This exercise gives actors an opportunity both to tell a story using few words and to use the powerful action of touching to help define character and relationship. The simple act of entwining fingers with a partner conveys a lot of information. Caution actors that gratuitous touching or keeping a hand on the other actor merely to be able to speak is not the purpose of the exercise. Encourage clever and logical methods of touching each other.

 ## Arms
(4 Actors)

Establish a scene. Have two actors put their hands behind their backs, and ask the remaining two actors to stand behind them and slip their arms through so their arms become the arms of the actors in front. The actors in front create the scene while the actors in back provide the arm movements.

DISCUSSION

Each arms/actor combination should be in sync. If they aren't, the character must justify why the arms have a mind of their own. If the speaking actors are greeting each other, the arms might shake hands, but if the arms suddenly grab the speaking actor's stomach, the character must justify the action. ("Oh, I ate to much!" "Yes, I'm six months pregnant." "Stewardess, do you have one of those 'special' paper bags?")

Second Thought
(2 Actors)

Establish a scene. As the scene progresses, call out one of the actor's names and say change. The actor whose name is called must change whatever he had planned to say next. In other words, the actor must have a second thought.

In Second Thought actors many times just say the opposite of what they had intended to say: "Gee, Kathleen you sure look [change] ugly tonight." The actor was about to say how nice the woman looked and switched to the negative version of the same thought. A second thought should be a completely different thought: "Gee, Kathleen you sure look [change] like you might win first prize with that iguana costume." Second Thought should prompt a where-did-that-come-from? reaction.

► ## *Emotion Jump*
(2 Actors)

Establish a scene. As the actors develop the scene, call out the name of one of the actors and identify an emotion or state of being. That actor's character must immediately assume the emotion or state of being and incorporate it into the scene. Throughout the scene, continue to change the emotions or states of being, alternating between actors.

EXAMPLES OF EMOTIONS/ STATES OF BEING

- Ecstatic
- Drunk
- Depressed
- Maniacal
- Cute
- Sarcastic
- Happy
- Birdlike
- Horny
- Tired
- Pissed off
- Sexy
- Vacuous
- Vindictive
- Weepy
- Snotty
- Wimpy
- Mute

DISCUSSION

In Emotion Jump it's very easy for an actor to become preoccupied with the constantly changing emotions and to forget to justify them within the context of the scene. A change of emotional state requires the actor to change the character's walk, mannerisms, way of speaking, way of dealing with relationships, etcetera. For example, being prissy means being prissy about *everything.* The actor would incorporate prissiness into every aspect of the character's demeanor. Make sure the actors continue to listen to each other and keep the story line moving forward even while dealing with the changing emotions.

▶ ## Emotion Transformation
(2 Actors)

Establish a scene and assign each actor a specific emotion to demonstrate. As the scene progresses, each actor must gradually assume the emotion of the other actor. The scene is over when the transformation is complete.

DISCUSSION

Emphasize the gradual transition from one emotion to the other.

▶ ## Second Emotion
(2 Actors)

Establish a scene and assign each actor two emotions or states of being. Each must begin with the first emotion and gradually make the transition to the second emotion, then end the scene.

DISCUSSION

Whereas in Emotion Jump the transition is abrupt, in both Emotion Transformation and Second Emotion it is the gradual nature of the emotional change that is important. Remind the actors that their emotional states must be consistent with the scene. If an actor begins the scene being joyful and ends it being angry, the dialogue, plot, and actions must support the transformation.

▶ Gibberish
(2 Actors)

Establish a scene and have the actors convey their meaning while speaking only gibberish.

DISCUSSION

Although gibberish is made up of nonsense words and should sound unintelligible, it is still an attempt to communicate. Encourage the actors to think in English but to express themselves in gibberish. Their inflections, actions, and gestures should help their scene partner understand what they are saying.

VARIATION

More advanced actors can add an accent to their gibberish, such as Japanese gibberish, Swiss gibberish, or Hawaiian gibberish. (This is good preparation for the Foreign Film exercise.)

▶ Translator
(2 Actors)

Establish an area of expertise as the scene's focus. One actor is an expert in this area but only speaks gibberish. The other actor must translate into English what the expert is saying.

DISCUSSION

Remind the actors speaking gibberish to pause after each line to provide time for the translation. Translator is also a good warm-up exercise for Foreign Film.

▶ *Gibberish Storytelling*
(Group Exercise)

Have one actor begin a story speaking gibberish. When characters (or trees, tables, houses, enchanted hedgehogs, whatever) are needed, have other actors go onstage and assume these identities. The storyteller must create a complete story, including a beginning, a middle, and an end. If any of the characters in the story speak, they must also do so in gibberish.

DISCUSSION

Unless the story is well known, this can be a challenging exercise. Remind the actors that by watching the storyteller and listening closely to the tone of the gibberish, they should be able to follow the story.

▶ *Get Them To*
(2 Actors)

This is an excellent exercise in coming up with choices and tactics to get what you want. Ask one actor to leave the room, and assign the remaining actor a task or a phrase. The second actor must get the first actor to perform the task or say the phrase—but by other means than simply asking the partner to do so. For example, if the second actor wants the first actor to kiss her hand, she might become the secretary of protocol in charge of rehearsing audiences with the Pope, or perhaps a Southern belle greeting a suitor. The tasks/phrases can be as simple as saying the word *Hispanic* or as complex as standing on a chair and acting like a chicken during mating season.

DISCUSSION

The actor must make strong choices about who, what, and where so that the objective is achieved (and an interesting scene created) without having to resort to blatant tactics.

 ## Rhyming Couplets
(Group Exercise)

Couplets are two consecutive lines of verse marked by rhythmic correspondence. Have the actors form a circle and ask one actor to create a poetic line. The next actor must comes up with a line in the same meter whose last word rhymes with the last word of the original line. The next actor provides the first line of a new couplet that continues the thought or idea, the next actor a line that rhymes with it, and so on around the circle.

DISCUSSION

You may go around the circle many times in this exercise. It sometimes helps to give the actors a topic or the title of a story to improvise. The idea of Rhyming Couplets is to develop a rhyming story, not just create indiscriminate rhyming verses.

Limericks
(Group Exercise)

Have the actors form a circle and ask one actor to create the first line of a limerick. (The limerick rhyme scheme is A, A, B, B, A). The next actor creates the second line (it rhymes with the first), the third actor the third line, and so on until the fifth actor finishes the limerick. Repeat the exercise until every actor has had the opportunity to create each line in the five-line series. Each limerick should make sense and tell a complete story.

EXAMPLE

ACTOR 1: There once was a bad guy named Sam,
ACTOR 2: A criminal out on the lam.
ACTOR 3: After one "job"
ACTOR 4: He squealed on the mob—
ACTOR 5: Now he's with the Witness Relocation Program.

DISCUSSION

The Limericks exercise is challenging because the actors must stay within a meter and a rhyme scheme (at least to some degree) and because each limerick must be a story with a beginning, a middle, and an end.

▶ Ask the Audience
(2 Actors)

Establish a scene. As the scene develops, call freeze at various times to stop the action. Have class members supply information the actors must then incorporate into their scene.

DISCUSSION

Ask the Audience offers good training in adaptability. Usually the best time to freeze the scene is after one of the actors has asked a question. This makes it easy for the audience to fill in the information. For example, if one of the actors asks, "So, Myron, where are you from?" you could freeze the scene and let someone say where Myron is from. If it's England, the actor playing Myron needs to assume an English accent, or explain why he doesn't have an English accent. Or if a wife says, "Honey, I'm going to lie down for a minute," you can freeze the action and ask, "Why is she going to lie down?" If the audience decides it's because the character is about to give birth, the actor must respond accordingly.

10 Advanced Exercises

► *Last Letter/Last Line*
(2 Actors)

Establish a scene. Ask the actors to begin every speech with a word that starts with the last letter of the last line given by the other actor. For example, if Actor 1 says, "Why Daphne, that party dress looks almost obscene!" Actor 2 must begin her line with a word that begins with *e*, since *obscene* ends in an *e*. "Edgar! My God, you're right! I have it on backward!" "Damned absentminded of you, Darling." "Good heavens, Edgar, have you looked at your pants?" And so on.

► *Entrance/Exit Words*
(4 Actors)

Before beginning this exercise, assign each actor an entrance/exit code word. Make sure all the actors know one another's code word. Establish a scene with two of the actors while the other two wait offstage. An actor can leave or enter the scene only when one of the other actors says that actor's code word. For example, an actor who's been give the code word *humid* cannot enter until another actor says that word. When the word is said again, the actor must find a reason to leave. An actor may say his own code word, but cannot use it to trigger an exit or an entrance.

Entrance/Exit Words is an excellent exercise to enhance listening and give-and-take between the actors. Remind the actors that their entrances or exits must be justified.

► *Slide Show*
(3 Actors)

Assign the actors a topic. One actor, acting as an expert on the topic, stands downstage from the other two actors. The two upstage actors act as "slides" the expert uses to illustrate the lecture. The expert introduces a slide while looking straight ahead, and the slide actors then strike a pose. Occasionally, the expert can turn to view the slide to help reinforce the point being made. The expert changes slides by saying, "In this next slide," and the slide actors then move into a new position and freeze.

Discussion

Slide Show is a good exercise for quick thinking. Have the expert try not to turn to look at the slide until there is a need to keep the lecture moving. At times the slides will help illustrate the speaker's point. At other times the speaker will have to think quickly to justify the slide. Use this exercise in conjunction with Expert.

► *Spotlight Scene*
(Group Exercise)

Tape out a five-feet-by-five-feet area center stage. This is the only area where dialogue can be heard, or "spotlighted." Begin with a group of six onstage actors, having them develop (in pairs) a scene in a place where people congregate (an office Christmas party, a grocery store, a museum, a sperm bank, etc.). Although all the actors are part of the scene and should participate in the action, only the pair of actors in the spotlighted area can be heard. Actors can stay in the spotlighted area until another pair of actors enter, then they must exit, continuing their scene inaudibly. Characters can return to the spotlighted area as often as they wish. Gradually increase the number of actors onstage until all actors are participating.

DISCUSSION

To avoid confusion and to prevent the actors from talking over one another, allow only two actors at a time in the spotlighted area. The actors outside this area need to listen to the speaking actors and use the information during their "moment in the spotlight." Scenes should flow easily from one to the other as actors enter and exit. Emphasize listening and give-and-take.

 ## Status
(3 Actors)

Establish a scene and assign each of the three actors a status. One actor has low status, another has middle status, and the third has high status. During the scene, the low-status actor must follow the instructions of both the other actors; the middle-status actor does only what the high-status actor demands; and the high-status actor controls the actions of the low-status and middle-status actors.

VARIATION

Call change and have the actors rotate status: low to middle, middle to high, and high to low.

DISCUSSION

Status is power. In a particular scene status may change or stay the same, depending on the actors' choices. For example, in a two-person scene between a boss and an employee, the characters can maintain traditional status assignments—boss–high, employee–low (the boss reviews the employee's performance, tells the employee what to do, or fires the employee)—or change their status many times— the employee has pictures of the boss with a nude woman (employee–high, boss–low); the nude woman turns out to be the boss's wife (employee–low, boss–high); the employee wins the lottery and buys the company (employee–high, boss–low); the boss is demoted to the employee's level (equal status).

▶ *Subtext*
(4 Actors)

Establish a scene. Have two of the actors improvise the scene; the two remaining actors sit offstage and, after each line of dialogue, say what the characters are really thinking. This subtext—the meaning underlying the dialogue—can be incorporated by the onstage actors during the scene.

EXAMPLE

ACTOR 1: You look lovely this evening, Lisa.
SUBTEXT 1: I wish I had the courage to kiss her.
ACTOR 2: Thank you, Norman. I had a nice time tonight.
SUBTEXT 2: If I go inside right now I can catch the end of *Casablanca.*

DISCUSSION

Remind the onstage actors that after they finish their lines they need to give the "subtext" actors time to voice their lines. This is a good listening and reacting exercise.

 ## *Playbook*
(2 Actors)

Establish a scene from an actual script (you'll need to provide a copy of the dialogue). Have one actor read a character's dialogue from the text while the other actor improvises the second character's part.

DISCUSSION

Even though at times the written dialogue will seem not to proceed logically, the improvising actor must try to justify *all* the dialogue in the scene.

VARIATION

Have the class call out a page number of a script, scene book, or anthology. Ask an actor to begin a scene using dialogue from that page while her partner improvises. The actor reading the text must use actual dialogue from the script but can pick and choose the lines she wants to use.

Abstract Scenes
(2 or More Actors)

Establish a scene and have the actors use abstract concepts to develop their improvisation.

- Two fish on a date.
- A museum with interacting art.
- Food going bad in a refrigerator.
- A sperm wooing an egg.

DISCUSSION

Abstract Scenes gives the actors a chance to use their three-dimensional thinking and quickly access their general knowledge. Where do fish go on a date? What do they do? (Go to a swim-in and see the horror film *Jaws?*) What if one is a devilfish, the other an angelfish? What if they are both sea horses? How does the fact that the male sea horse gives birth to the babies affect the date?

After the exercise, have the class brainstorm different ideas, traits, facts, and behaviors that might have been useful to the actors. This is one of the reasons it is important that actors read. In improvisation, knowledge truly is power. The more information actors have at their fingertips, the more interesting the choices available to them.

▶ *Animal Images*
(1 Actor)

Assign each actor (or have each actor choose) an animal to portray. Without making animal sounds, each actor must emulate the animal, capturing its movement and energy.

DISCUSSION

We constantly use animal images in our speech: she eats like a horse (or a bird), he's as fat as a pig (or as wise as an owl), she's a dog, he's a snake, she's an eager beaver, they hump like bunnies. Actors frequently use animal images as a way to add different rhythms, movements, and qualities to their characterizations. Famous examples include Dustin Hoffman's Ratso Rizzo in *Midnight Cowboy;* Marlon Brando's man/ape in *A Streetcar Named Desire;* Danny DeVito's Penguin and Michelle Pfieffer's Catwoman in *Batman Returns.*

The first step in creating a character based on an animal is to explore the animal's physicality. Have the actors not only sit and walk like the animal, but stretch, hunt or be hunted, preen, and become angry like the animal. Exploring the animal's movements and behaviors can give the actors insight into the essence of the animal. Sometimes I give this exercise as homework so the actors can research the animal. In portraying a dog, it isn't enough to lift a leg at a tree or a fire hydrant (if it's a male dog; female dogs squat). An actor must know the species of the animal. Eagles and flamingos are both birds, but they move, eat, and fly very differently.

▶ *Animal Evolution*
(1 Actor)

Have the actor portray an animal. Ask her to enter from one side of the stage and as she walks slowly across the stage to evolve from the animal into a human being.

DISCUSSION

Remind the actors to take their time with the transformation and to discover how the animal's movement changes into human movement.

► *Animal Interviews*
(1 Actor)

Have one actor sit onstage and be interviewed by the class. The actor, though portraying a human being, must answer the questions based on an image of a specific animal. Answering questions like What is your name? What do you do for a living? Where do you live? Who do you most admire? gives the actor a chance to work on abstract thinking.

DISCUSSION

What kind of job would a human cockroach have? (Garbage collector? Night security guard?) Where might a human lion work? (I have an office in my den.) How does a human chicken kiss?

In one class an actor decided to be a cat. During the interview we found out her character was born in Siam, her name was Felicia, she was fond of sushi, was once bitten by a dog (and is now frightened of them), came from a big family (though she hasn't seen them in years), and has had many sexual partners. She sat very gracefully with her legs and her eyes crossed, affecting an air of sophistication. She was the personification of a Siamese cat, to the point of coughing as if she had a hairball.

VARIATION

Try this exercise as a guessing game. Rather than identifying the animal beforehand, have the class guess the animal.

► *Humanimals*
(2 Actors)

Establish a scene and have the actors develop it as characters who are the human version of animals.

DISCUSSION

You may want to assign the actors animals that will create conflict—a mouse–waitress and a cat–customer, a used-car salesman–snake and a mongoose–boss, a loan shark and a remora buddy, a good-looking chicken on a date with a wolf.

▶ *Animal Dance*
(Group Exercise)

Have the actors portray humanized animals at a dance. The animals can all be the same species or different species.

DISCUSSION

Animal Dance, like Spotlight Scene, should be set up by taping out an acting area. It is only when the animals dance into the spotlighted area that their dialogue can be heard.

▶ *Foreign Film*
(4 Actors)

Have two actors create a scene from a foreign-language film. These actors speak only in gibberish while the two remaining actors translate the dialogue into English. Make sure the actors speaking gibberish allow time for the translation after each line of dialogue.

DISCUSSION

Remind the actors to listen to one another and to be aware that the translators may be conveying a different story line. For example, while the actors are doing a gibberish version of *Hansel and Gretel*, the translators may be rendering the dialogue as if it's from an Ingmar Bergman film.

▶ *Dubbing*
  (4 Actors)

Have two actors create a scene from a foreign-language film. The two onstage actors move their lips while the two remaining actors supply their voices. The dubbing actors should try to synchronize the dialogue with the mouth movements of the onstage actors.

DISCUSSION

Remind the onstage actors to keep the scene physically interesting. It is important that the onstage actors and the dubbing actors work together to create a story. This exercise and Foreign Film are also helpful in practicing foreign accents and dialects. Vocal Mirror and Twins are good warm-ups for this exercise.

▶ *Genre/Style Change*
  (2 or More Actors)

Have the class list different genres of film, television, theatre, books, different directorial styles, different authors, etcetera. Establish a scene. As the scene progresses call out the different genres. The actors must immediately adapt the scene to the changing styles.

EXAMPLES

- Murder mystery
- Commercial
- Musical comedy
- Puppet show
- Farce
- Horror film

- Children's show
- Shakespeare
- Tennessee Williams
- Cartoon
- Science fiction
- Romantic comedy

- Porno film
- Talk show
- Infomercial
- Alfred Hitchcock
- Medical show
- Soap opera
- Sporting event

- High school play
- National Geographic special
- Situation comedy
- Dance concert
- Commedia Dell'Arte
- Farm report
- Theatre in the round

DISCUSSION

Genre/Style Change is a staple of improvisational comedy groups, and is also a valuable exercise for the actor. Remind the actors to try to capture the essence of the style or genre. If a husband and wife are driving to the Grand Canyon in a scene à la Tennessee Williams, the actors might say (in a southern dialect) "How much farther is it, Stanley?" "Damn it, Stella! Will you quit askin' that?" Switching to soap opera: "I'm sorry Stanley, it's just I can't stop thinking about Blanche." "You mean your sister I raped and sent over the edge?" Switching to medical show: "Sent over the edge? Dr. Kowalski, I believe it was more in the nature of a deterioration of mental faculties combined with emotional disturbances, resulting from organic brain disorder." "Of course you're right, Stella." And so on.

Let the scenes progress longer than the couple of sentences used here as examples. The most difficult part of this exercise is to remain true to the changing styles while continuing to move the scene forward.

▶ *Two Scenes*
(4 Actors)

Divide the stage in half and have two of the actors stand stage right and the remaining two actors stand stage left. Have each pair of actors establish a scene (the two scenes may or may not relate to each other). The actors stage right begin their scene. As the scene progresses, the actors stage left begin talking and draw the focus to their scene. The stage-right actors freeze in place. After the stage-left scene proceeds awhile, the stage-right actors take the focus back by resuming their scene at the point they left off.

DISCUSSION

Two Scenes is a wonderful exercise to rehearse give-and-take. One scene shouldn't dominate the exercise. The actors must be alert not only to what is happening in their scene but to what is happening in the other scene as well.

► ## Two Scenes with Activator
(5 Actors)

This exercise is conducted the same way as Two Scenes but includes a fifth person, who "activates" the scenes. After the scenes are established, the stage-right scene begins. The activator takes part in the scene but can leave it at any time, cross the center line dividing the scenes, and activate the stage-left scene by entering it. The stage-right actors must then freeze until the activator reenters their scene. The activator goes back and forth at will, interacting with both scenes.

DISCUSSION

The activator doesn't need to justify leaving a scene. When the activator leaves the scene—even if it's in the middle of someone else's line—that scene freezes and the other scene is activated.

VARIATION 1

Give all the actors in the exercise the ability to be the activator. Any one of the actors in the three-person scene can leave that scene and activate the other scene. Scene partners thus constantly change.

VARIATION 2

The activator must justify both departing from a scene and entering the other scene.

► *Two Scenes/Last Word*
(4 Actors)

Conduct this exercise like Two Scenes. When the actors draw the focus to their scene, they must do so with a line of dialogue that begins with the last word spoken in the other scene.

EXAMPLE

Let's say that the stage-right dialogue is "Of course you're right, Danielle, that bastard must die." An actor in the stage-left scene then switches the focus to that scene with a line beginning with the last word: "Die you lousy cockroaches! Hank, hand me your shoe!" The scenes switch back and forth, each being true to its story line but taking focus with a line that begins with the last word spoken in the other scene.

DISCUSSION

Give each scene some time to develop; the focus shouldn't be switched too quickly.

► *Two Scenes/Last Letter*
(4 Actors)

This exercise is conducted the same way as Two Scenes/Last Word but is even more challenging. When the actors in the inactive scene want to take focus, they must start the dialogue with a word that begins with the last letter of the last word spoken in the other scene.

DISCUSSION

In all the Two Scenes exercises, listening is of utmost importance. Try using the Last Letter Slap-Clap-Snap, Alphabet Scene, and Last Letter/Last Line exercises as warm-ups.

► *Three Characters*
(3 Actors)

Establish a scene. Two actors begin the scene, eventually talking about a third character, who then enters the scene. The third actor must take on all the character attributes discussed by the first two actors in the beginning of the scene.

DISCUSSION

Sometimes actors find out more about their character from the other characters' lines than from their own. This exercise provides the opportunity to build a character based on information supplied by the other characters.

► *Three Scenes*
(6 Actors)

Have the actors work in pairs, with one pair stage left, one pair center stage, and one pair stage right. Don't establish a scene or provide any other information. Ask the stage-right actors to begin a scene, the only requirement being that during it they must mention other characters or events. When you call change, the center actors begin a scene using information from the first scene. When you call change again, the stage-left actors begin a scene using information from both of the other scenes. Continue to change the scenes, having the actors incorporate the information they are gathering from the other scenes.

▶ Variations on a Theme
(Group Exercise)

Select a broad theme for the exercise—love, revenge, childhood, marriage, sports, dating, the history of sex, science, etc. From then on it's a free-for-all. Have the actors take turns improvising scenes and/or monologues based on the selected theme. The scenes and monologues should be short but should clearly indicate who, where, and what. The actors should be ready to jump in with a new scene or monologue as soon as a scene or monologue reaches its peak.

▶ Tribes
(Group Exercise)

Tell the actors that they are members of an aboriginal tribe with their own customs, social structure, and language (gibberish). Ask them to develop a scene that represents one day in the life of the tribe. The exercise begins as the sun rises and the tribe members wake; it ends at night, when the tribe members go to sleep.

DISCUSSION

This is a fascinating exercise both to watch and to be involved in. Designed for advanced actors, it can take anywhere from thirty minutes to two hours. It's better to do very little side coaching, but do announce changes in the time of day (sunrise, noon, sunset) so the participants can adjust the scene accordingly. Take notes on what you observe during the exercise. Watch which actors become workers, warriors, leaders, followers, religious leaders, and how relationships develop and social status is taken and given. Observe how the environment develops and where fires, sleeping areas, altars, streams, trees, are placed. Be very aware of the tribe's "language"—how it is used, and whether words are picked up by the other members of the tribe. You may be surprised at how well the actors work together to create a fully realized improvisation.

IMPORTANT

The Tribes improvisation can become very physical. Make it absolutely clear to the actors that no person may strike another during the exercise.

▶ *Make a Play*
(Group Exercise)

Have the actors improvise a half-hour play based on an invented title.

DISCUSSION

I sometimes divide the class into smaller groups and have each group improvise a play rather than do the exercise with the entire class. Whichever way you do it, before attempting this exercise, remind the actors that not everyone can have a starring role. The objective of this exercise is for the actors to develop an improvised play as a group. They should listen to one another, work together, and create a plot that includes many characters and that can continue for an extended period of time.

▶ Soundtrack
(2 or More Actors)

Have each actor tape a two-minute portion of any type of music (you could also use a rehearsal pianist). Play one of the tapes for the class and have a group of two or more actors create a completely mimed scene based on the music. The actions in the scene must convey who, what, and where.

Discussion

Remind the actors that although the music will set a mood and will give a feel to the scene, they can choose to create a scene that is counter to that mood if they wish. Two minutes of the finale of "The 1812 Overture" might lead as easily to a scene about two teenagers falling in love as to a scene in which two adults argue over a divorce settlement.

Variation

Have the actors speak in the scene.

▶ Opera
(2 or More Actors)

Establish a scene in which all the action will be underscored with music and all the dialogue must be sung. The music should enhance and reflect the action and dialogue developed during the scene.

Discussion

This exercise requires a rehearsal pianist who can improvise. It's fun to do, especially for actors familiar with operatic style and plots, and is also a good introduction to improvised singing. Because the lyrics need not rhyme, the actors can concentrate on their voices and on creating a plot furthered by the dialogue-lyrics. (The difficulty increases dramatically when the actors have to rhyme.) Encourage the pianist to vary the tempo, mood, and style of the music to enhance the scene.

▶ Songmaker
(1 or More Actors)

Give the actor a title for a song. A rehearsal pianist (or guitarist) begins to improvise an original song based on this title, and the actor improvises lyrics. Repeat the exercise to include solos, duets, trios, and group numbers.

DISCUSSION

A great singing voice is not necessary for this exercise. Instruct the pianist to choose simple, repeatable chord progressions in early attempts to create songs. Have the actors warm up for this exercise by doing Rhyming Couplets and Limericks.

▶ Musical Scenes
(2 or More Actors)

Establish a scene. During the scene, the actors are to lead up to a song and give the song cue. A pianist will then begin playing an original piece of improvised music, and the actors must sing the song. Ideally, the scene should flow into the song and the song should flow back into the scene.

DISCUSSION

As with Songmaker, the actors don't need great singing voices, but it helps to have a good knowledge of musicals and musical styles. Instruct the pianist to choose simple, repeatable chord progressions in early attempts to create songs. Because most songs in musicals rhyme, good warm-ups for this exercise are Rhyming Couplets, Limericks, and Songmaker.

▶ *Musicals*
(Group Exercise)

Make up a title for a musical. Ask two actors, backed by an improvisational rehearsal pianist, to develop a scene based on this title. Have the entire class gradually join the scene, creating a full-length musical. The musical should have a chorus, numerous songs, improvised dance numbers, solos, duets, trios, and production numbers.

DISCUSSION

This is a very advanced exercise, but don't let that scare you. If the actors have previously worked on Make a Play, Songmaker, and Musical Scenes, they will have developed the skills they need to create a musical. And remember: the more often actors rehearse the exercises in this book, the easier they become.

The Next Step

Now that you've read this book, understood the concepts, perfected the exercises, and perhaps taught them to others, you can sit back and wait for your Improvisational Actor Certificate of Merit to come in the mail. Right?

Wrong.

The best actors continuously work at their craft. When you stop working at being a better actor, atrophy quickly sets in. Your memory becomes fuzzy, your reactions slow down, and you find yourself walking out of every audition and every performance feeling that you didn't do your best. And to be honest, you didn't.

It is obvious that dancers must constantly work to keep their body in shape and that singers must keep their voice in tip-top condition. Even doctors, who spend *years* training for their profession, must keep abreast of the latest medical techniques. Why should it be any different for professional actors?

Acting, improvisation, being an actor, never stops. This is why successful television, stage, and film actors still read books, take classes, and teach workshops. After you've gotten everything you can out of this book, read another (try Viola Spolin's *Improvisation for the Theater* or any number of other acting books in the library). Sign up for an improv class (hell, *organize* an improv class with your fellow actors and use this book as your guide). Use your new skills at your next audition or rehearsal. The point is, just do it! Actors never stop training, experiencing, learning, experimenting, trying, failing, succeeding, improvising, and growing. Improvisation is just one more skill you need in your acting arsenal. The more you know, the more interesting you'll be, and interesting people make interesting actors. The world can't keep its eyes off intelligent, creative, interesting actors!

 # Fifteen Sample Classes

The sample classes that follow are designed to suggest when concepts should be introduced. They represent general ways to structure a class and begin training an actor in improvisation. Please don't feel tied to the specific exercises under these broad headings.

Also, the fifteen sample classes given here don't include every exercise in this book. Because each actor and each class is different, you will need to modify your classes to meet the actors' needs. Move the exercises around to create classes that will provide the particular actors in them the most benefit.

For example, if you have a small class, the Name Volleyball exercise might not be helpful, so use Name Cheer instead, or pick a trust exercise. You will eventually identify the exercises that you feel are important and that work well with your style of teaching.

These suggested sample classes are designed with the assumption that each class will last from two to three hours. If you have an ideal class size (ten actors), you might get to all of the exercises that are outlined for one class. Chances are, however, that your class will be larger and fewer exercises will be used (I've taught classes with forty students in which I was lucky to do three exercises). Take your time with the exercises and allow each actor to try them *at least*

twice. The exercises should be repeated as often as necessary to build proficiency.

▶ *Class 1—Introduction to Improvisation*

WARM-UPS
Oooh-Aaah
Last Letter Slap-Clap-Snap
Counting
Simon Sez

EXERCISES
Name with Action
Name Volleyball
I/My Interview
Personal Commercial
Introduction Circle

▶ *Class 2—Trust/Ensemble*

WARM-UPS
Oooh-Aaah
Last Letter Slap-Clap-Snap
Name Six
One-Word Story
Continuing Story

EXERCISES
Expert
Halftime Show
Group Mime
Trust Circle
Honey Walk

▶ Class 3—Trust/Ensemble

WARM-UPS
Oooh-Aaah
Name Six
Last Letter Slap-Clap-Snap
One-Word Story
Continuing Story
A-B-C Circle

EXERCISES
Trust Run
Mirror
Changing Mirror
Vocal Mirror
Listening Argument
Hitchhiker

▶ Class 4—Introduction of Who, What, Where, When, Why, How

WARM-UPS
Oooh-Aaah
Name Six Plus
Last Letter Slap-Clap-Snap
Word Association
One-Word Story
A-B-C Circle
Energy Circle
Obstacle Course

EXERCISES
Freeze Tag
The Bus Stop

Where Are We?
Six Scenes
Neutral Scenes

▶ Class 5—Emphasis on Quick Thinking/Mental Agility/Abstract Thinking

WARM-UPS
Oooh-Aaah
Name Six
A-B-C Circle
Diamond Follow-the-Leader
What Would You Be If?
Supernova

EXERCISES
Freeze
This Is Not a Stick
Model/Artist/Clay
Machines and Variations
Alphabet Scene

▶ Class 6—Emphasis on Who

WARM-UPS
Oooh-Aaah
Hot Subject
Last Letter Slap-Clap-Snap Variation
Word Association
Head Holding
In Everyone's Life
Family Portraits

EXERCISES
Three-Character Interview
Touching
Age Walk
Family Reunion
This Is Your Life

► Class 7—Emphasis on Where

WARM-UPS
Oooh-Aaah
Name Six Plus
Word Association
Who's the Leader?
Backtalk
Commercial

EXERCISES
Where Are You Going?
Where Were You?
Set the Mood
Entrance/Exit Words

■ Class 8—Emphasis on What

WARM-UPS
Oooh-Aaah
Name Six Plus
Hot Subject
Last Letter Slap-Clap-Snap Variation
In Everyone's Life
Changing Ball Toss

Object Transformation
One-Word History
Constant Action
Specifics
Subtext

▶ *Class 9—Emphasis on Choices*

WARM-UPS
Oooh-Aaah
Name Six Plus
Hot Subject
Last Letter Slap-Clap-Snap Variation
Hunter/Hunted

EXERCISES
No, It's Not
Surprise Prop
Second Thought
Get Them To
Arms
Abstract Scenes

▶ *Class 10—Playwriting*

WARM-UPS
Oooh-Aaah
Name Six Plus
Hot Subject
One-Word Interview
Sixty-Second Movie

EXERCISES
First Line/Last Line
Beginning/Middle/End
Beginning/Middle/End Variations
Past/Present/Future

▶ *Class 11—Playwriting*

WARM-UPS
Oooh-Aaah
Last Letter Slap-Clap-Snap
One-Word History
Continuing Story
Murderer

EXERCISES
No Questions
Before and After
Storytelling
Storytelling with Sound Effects
Tag-Team Storytellers

▶ *Class 12—Give-and-Take*

WARM-UPS
Oooh-Aaah
Last Letter Slap-Clap-Snap
Word Association
Debate
Obstacle Course

One Line Each
Status
Two Scenes
Two Scenes with Activator
Two Scenes/Last Word
Dubbing

▶ *Class 13—Gibberish*

WARM-UPS
Oooh-Aaah
Last Letter Slap-Clap-Snap
Name Six
Twins
Energy Circle

EXERCISES
Gibberish
Translator
Gibberish Storytelling
Foreign Film

▶ *Class 14—Emotion*

WARM-UPS
Oooh-Aaah
Last Letter Slap-Clap-Snap
Continuing Styles
Face Touch

EXERCISES
Emotion Jump
Emotion Transformation
Second Emotion
Moment of Crisis

► *Class 15—Playwriting*

WARM-UPS
Oooh-Aaah
Name Six Plus
Continuing Styles
Mormon Tabernacle Freeze

EXERCISES
Three Scenes
Ask the Audience
Variations on a Theme
Playbook
Tribes

Even though each class outline has a specific emphasis, keep reinforcing all elements of improvisation in every class. Since these exercises work on many different levels—a where exercise can just as easily be used to help an actor create a strong who, when, or what—don't limit yourself to working on only one aspect of an exercise.

Again, repeat the exercises as needed and take your time working each one. And, as always, when in doubt—improvise!

B Solving Common Problems

Listed here are some of the common problems that beginning improvisational actors face and specific exercises to help solve them. You will notice that some of the exercises can be used to solve a variety of problems.

If you tend to be a linear thinker, these exercises help you think on a more abstract level:

Freeze Tag
What Would You Be If?
This Is Not a Stick
Object Transformation
Abstract Scenes
Humanimals
Playbook
Slide Show
Machines
Second Thought
Subtext
Variations on a Theme
Soundtrack

If you need help in making stronger choices:

Charades
In Everyone's Life

Specifics
Get Them To
No Questions
Storytelling
Genre/Style Change
Moment of Crisis
Emotion Jump
Status
Subtext
This Is Your Life

If you have trouble allowing other actors in a scene to make choices:

Obstacle Course
Diamond Follow-the-Leader
Hitchhiker
Neutral Scenes
Status
Entrance/Exit Words
Get Them To
Alphabet Scene
Dubbing
This Is Your Life
Storytelling
Tag-Team Storytellers
One Line Each

If you tend to preconceive:

Oooh-Aaah
Last Letter Slap-Clap-Snap
Continuing Story
Name Six
Name Six Plus
Hot Subject

One-Word Story
Word Association
A-B-C Circle
Alphabet Scene
Mirror
Vocal Mirror
Ask the Audience
No, It's Not
Freeze
Freeze Tag
Second Thought

If you need to enhance your concentration:

Last Letter Slap-Clap-Snap
Name Six
Concentration
A-B-C Circle
Blind Walk
Changing Ball Toss
Mirror
Changing Mirror
Vocal Mirror
Listening Argument
Debate
Simon Sez
Word Association
Energy Circle
Hand-Clap Circle
Twins
One-Word Story
One-Word Interview
One-Word History
Continuing Story
Continuing Styles

Constant Action
Storytelling
Two Scenes
Two Scenes/Last Word
Two Scenes/Last Letter
Entrance/Exit Words
Three Characters
Three Scenes
Dubbing
Foreign Film
Playbook

If you overtalk in your scenes, never letting your partner get a word in:

One-Word History
One-Word Story
One-Word Interview
Vocal Mirror
One Line Each
Neutral Scenes
Alphabet Scene
Dubbing
Foreign Film
Playbook
Subtext
Before and After

If you need to speed up your thought processes:

Oooh-Aaah
Rabbit/Duck/Elephant
Name Six
Name Six Plus
Hot Subject
A-B-C Circle

Word Association
Listening Argument
Expert
Debate
Commercial
Family Portraits
Simon Sez
This Is Not a Stick
Continuing Story
Continuing Styles
No, It's Not
No Questions
Second Thought
Subtext
Rhyming Couplets
Limericks
Songmaker
Three-Character Interview
Ask the Audience

If you just sit and talk during your scenes:

Age Walk
Freeze Tag
Freeze
Vocal Mirror
Animal Evolution
Constant Action
Touching
Three Objects
Family Reunion
Family Vacation
Entrance/Exit Words
Spotlight Scene
Two Scenes with Activator

If your mime is sloppy:

> This Is Not a Stick
> Group Mime
> Object Transformation
> Changing Ball Toss
> Constant Action
> Surprise Prop
> Three Objects
> Arms
> Tribes

If you have trouble making a physical connection with your partner:

> Mirror
> Energy Circle
> Hand-Clap Circle
> Trust Fall
> Head Holding
> Machines
> Face Touch
> Touching
> Slide Show
> Animal Dance
> Arms

If you need to get energized:

> Oooh-Aaah
> Name Six
> Trust Run
> Rabbit/Duck/Elephant
> Simon Sez
> Hand-Clap Circle
> Energy Circle
> Supernova

Sixty-Second Movie
Freeze Tag
Emotion Jump
Three-Character Interview

If the class is not working together as an ensemble:

One-Word Story
One-Word History
Mirror
Vocal Mirror
Group Roll
Group Mime
Diamond Follow-the-Leader
Family Portraits
Mormon Tabernacle Freeze
Machines
Hand-Clap Circle
Beginning/Middle/End
Storytelling
Make a Play
Tribes
Spotlight Scene
Animal Dance
Variations on a Theme
This Is Your Life
Rhyming Couplets
Limericks
Musical Scenes

If you need to work on your listening skills:

Simon Sez
Word Association
Last Letter Slap-Clap-Snap
Vocal Mirror

Listening Argument
Twins
One-Word Story
One-Word Interview
One-Word History
Continuing Story
Continuing Styles
Beginning/Middle/End
Past/Present/Future
Storytelling
Storytelling with Sound Effects
Tag-Team Storytellers
Two Scenes
Two Scenes/Last Word
Two Scenes/Last Letter
Entrance/Exit Words
Three Characters
Three Scenes
Dubbing
Foreign Film
Soundtrack
Playbook

If you need help establishing who/character:

Age Walk
Hitchhiker
Twins
Six Scenes
Family Reunion
Neutral Scenes
Three-Character Interview
Before and After
Costume Pieces
Three Characters

Three Scenes
This Is Your Life
Beginning/Middle/End
Past/Present/Future
Humanimals
Animal Dance
Animal Evolution
Genre/Style Change
Tribes
Make a Play
Opera
Musical Scenes
Musicals

If you need help establishing where/setting:

Honey Walk
Six Scenes
Where Are We?
Where Were You?
Where Are You Going?
The Bus Stop
Neutral Scenes
Family Vacation
Whisper/Normal/Shout
Specifics
Surprise Prop
Two Scenes
Two Scenes with Activator
Three Scenes
Tribes
Make a Play
Opera
Musical Scenes
Musicals

If you need help establishing when/time:

Age Walk
Six Scenes
The Bus Stop
Neutral Scenes
Costume Pieces
This Is Your Life
Beginning/Middle/End
Past/Present/Future
Genre/Style Change
Storytelling
Soundtrack

If you need help establishing what/plot:

Freeze Tag
Freeze
One-Word Story
Continuing Story
Continuing Styles
Experts
Rhyming Couplets
Limericks
Six Scenes
Neutral Scenes
Sixty-Second Movie
This Is Your Life
First Line/Last Line
Beginning/Middle/End
Before and After
Storytelling
Storytelling with Sound Effects
Tag-Team Storytellers
Ask the Audience

Genre/Style Change
Playbook
Tribes
Make a Play
Opera
Songmaker
Musical Scenes
Musicals

If you need help establishing why/motivation:

Freeze Tag
Freeze
Mormon Tabernacle Freeze
Six Scenes
Neutral Scenes
Whisper/Normal/Shout
Second Thought
Ask the Audience
No, It's Not
Subtext
Genre/Style Change
Before and After
Three Characters
Entrance/Exit Words
Three Scenes
Slide Show
Get Them To
Soundtrack
Musical Scenes
Make a Play
Musicals

If you need help establishing how/action:

Six Scenes
Neutral Scenes

Get Them To
Three Objects
Constant Action
Touching
Arms
First Line/Last Line
Emotional Transformation
Gibberish
Status
Genre/Style Change
Variations on a Theme
Soundtrack
Tribes
Make a Play
Constant Action
Arms